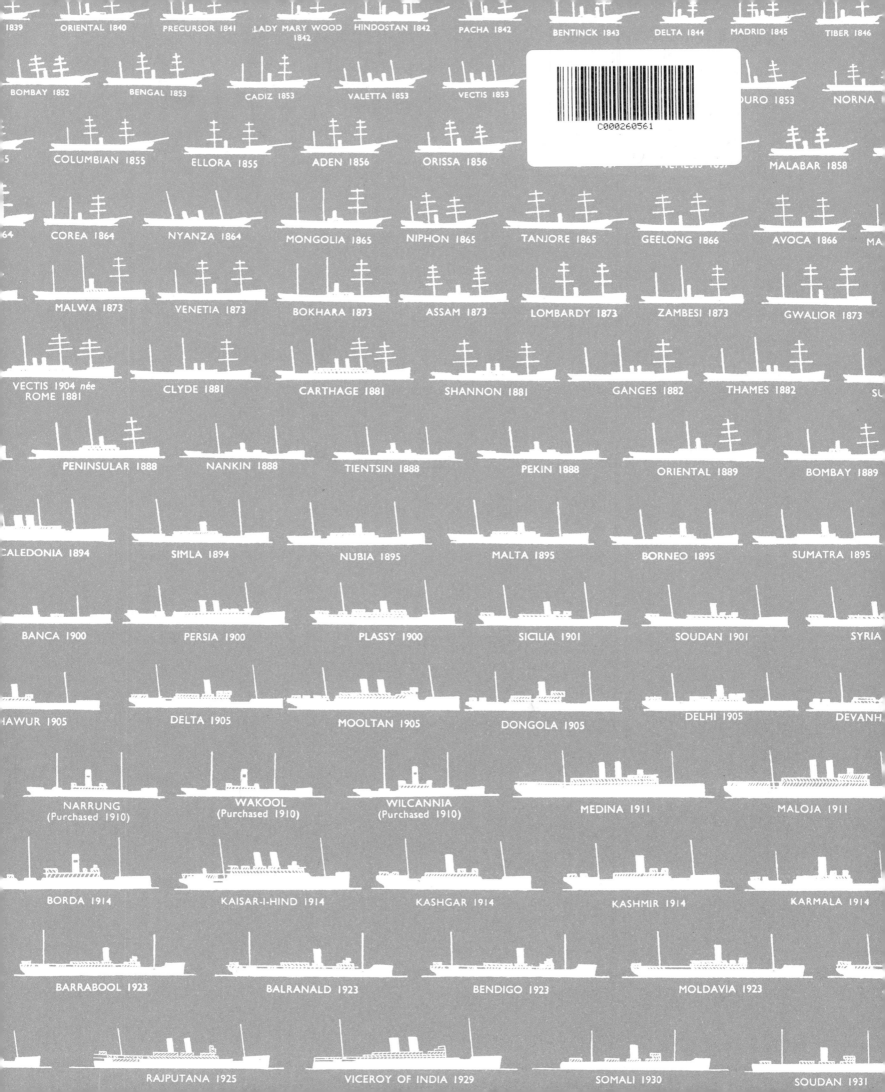

1839 ORIENTAL 1840 PRECURSOR 1841 LADY MARY WOOD 1842 HINDOSTAN 1842 PACHA 1842 BENTINCK 1843 DELTA 1844 MADRID 1845 TIBER 1846

BOMBAY 1852 BENGAL 1853 CADIZ 1853 VALETTA 1853 VECTIS 1853 DURO 1853 NORNA

COLUMBIAN 1855 ELLORA 1855 ADEN 1856 ORISSA 1856 NEMESIS 1857 MALABAR 1858

COREA 1864 NYANZA 1864 MONGOLIA 1865 NIPHON 1865 TANJORE 1865 GEELONG 1866 AVOCA 1866 MA

MALWA 1873 VENETIA 1873 BOKHARA 1873 ASSAM 1873 LOMBARDY 1873 ZAMBESI 1873 GWALIOR 1873

VECTIS 1904 née ROME 1881 CLYDE 1881 CARTHAGE 1881 SHANNON 1881 GANGES 1882 THAMES 1882 SU

PENINSULAR 1888 NANKIN 1888 TIENTSIN 1888 PEKIN 1888 ORIENTAL 1889 BOMBAY 1889

CALEDONIA 1894 SIMLA 1894 NUBIA 1895 MALTA 1895 BORNEO 1895 SUMATRA 1895

BANCA 1900 PERSIA 1900 PLASSY 1900 SICILIA 1901 SOUDAN 1901 SYRIA

HAWUR 1905 DELTA 1905 MOOLTAN 1905 DONGOLA 1905 DELHI 1905 DEVANH

NARRUNG (Purchased 1910) WAKOOL (Purchased 1910) WILCANNIA (Purchased 1910) MEDINA 1911 MALOJA 1911

BORDA 1914 KAISAR-I-HIND 1914 KASHGAR 1914 KASHMIR 1914 KARMALA 1914

BARRABOOL 1923 BALRANALD 1923 BENDIGO 1923 MOLDAVIA 1923

RAJPUTANA 1925 VICEROY OF INDIA 1929 SOMALI 1930 SOUDAN 1931

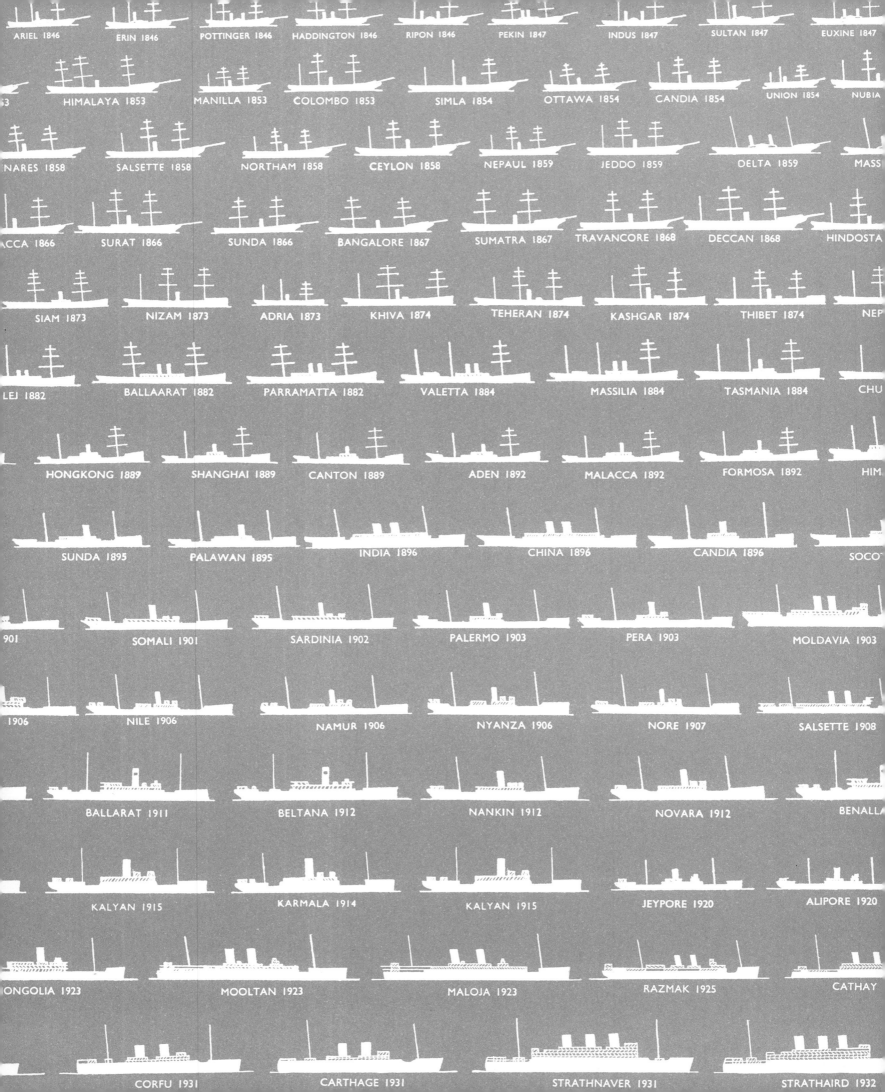

ARIEL 1846   ERIN 1846   POTTINGER 1846   HADDINGTON 1846   RIPON 1846   PEKIN 1847   INDUS 1847   SULTAN 1847   EUXINE 1847

53   HIMALAYA 1853   MANILLA 1853   COLOMBO 1853   SIMLA 1854   OTTAWA 1854   CANDIA 1854   UNION 1854   NUBIA

NARES 1858   SALSETTE 1858   NORTHAM 1858   CEYLON 1858   NEPAUL 1859   JEDDO 1859   DELTA 1859   MASS

ACCA 1866   SURAT 1866   SUNDA 1866   BANGALORE 1867   SUMATRA 1867   TRAVANCORE 1868   DECCAN 1868   HINDOSTA

SIAM 1873   NIZAM 1873   ADRIA 1873   KHIVA 1874   TEHERAN 1874   KASHGAR 1874   THIBET 1874   NEP

LEJ 1882   BALLAARAT 1882   PARRAMATTA 1882   VALETTA 1884   MASSILIA 1884   TASMANIA 1884   CHU

HONGKONG 1889   SHANGHAI 1889   CANTON 1889   ADEN 1892   MALACCA 1892   FORMOSA 1892   HIM

SUNDA 1895   PALAWAN 1895   INDIA 1896   CHINA 1896   CANDIA 1896   SOCO

901   SOMALI 1901   SARDINIA 1902   PALERMO 1903   PERA 1903   MOLDAVIA 1903

1906   NILE 1906   NAMUR 1906   NYANZA 1906   NORE 1907   SALSETTE 1908

BALLARAT 1911   BELTANA 1912   NANKIN 1912   NOVARA 1912   BENALL

KALYAN 1915   KARMALA 1914   KALYAN 1915   JEYPORE 1920   ALIPORE 1920

ONGOLIA 1923   MOOLTAN 1923   MALOJA 1923   RAZMAK 1925   CATHAY

CORFU 1931   CARTHAGE 1931   STRATHNAVER 1931   STRATHAIRD 1932

ACROSS THE OCEANS
ACROSS THE YEARS

ACROSS THE OCEANS
ACROSS THE YEARS

A Pictorial Voyage

Ruth Artmonsky

Susie Cox

Antique Collectors' Club

P&O Across the Oceans, Across the Years
A Pictorial Voyage

© 2012 P&OSNCo.
www.poheritage.com

ISBN 978 1 85149 691 4

British Library cataloguing-in-publication data.
A catalogue record for this book is available from
the British Library.

Antique Collectors' Club
www.antiquecollectorsclub.com
Sandy Lane, Old Martlesham,
Woodbridge, Suffolk, 1P12 4SD, UK
Tel: 01394 389950 Fax: 01394 389999
Email: info@antique-acc.com

ACC Distribution
6 West, 18th Street, Suite 4B
New York, NY 10011
Tel: 212 645 1111 Fax: 212 989 3205
Email: sales@antiquecc.com

Published in England by the Antique
Collectors' Club, Woodbridge, Suffolk.

Designed by Webb & Webb Design Ltd.
Printed and bound in England by Empress Litho
on FSC certified paper.

ACKNOWLEDGEMENTS

This book could not have been written without the totally committed help
of P&O Heritage. I would like to acknowledge not only the many hours
they voluntarily gave to the selection of the images and to digging out
relevant written material, but to the very real interest and diligence they
applied to the editing of the final text. It was one of those delightful
occasions when curator and author, with common aims, work as a team.
RUTH ARTMONSKY

My heartfelt thanks go to Ruth who has infected us all with her inestimable
energy, enthusiasm and talents, and to Beth Ellis and Anna-Klara Hahn,
from P&O Heritage, for working tirelessly and way beyond their watch.
My sincere thanks go to Stephen Rabson for his expertise, to Simon Ball for
indexing, Marc Walter and Sabine Arque-Greenberg for photography and to
Sarah Lockie from DP World and James Smith of Antique Collectors' Club for
their much valued support. Special thanks go to Brian Webb and Dan Smith of
Webb & Webb for working their magic and producing a beautiful book.

At P&O Heritage we are indebted to those who have collected before us and
those who have over many years been kind enough to donate their diaries,
letters, photographs, ephemera and mementoes, or those of their families.
It is these glimpses into the human story of P&O that breathe life into our
collections and our past. Thanks to the generosity of Anne Dunkley, we
count among these the archives of her late father, who served P&O for
almost fifty years. Not only has Commodore Dunkley become the 'pin-up'
in our office, his albums, filled as they are with humour and joyful days at
sea, remind us that P&O was a way of life – a fun one at that.

Finally, we are enormously privileged to work with an exceptional collection
that owes its existence to a joy and a pride in the history of P&O and its
preservation today, to the generosity and commitment of its equally proud
owners, DP World.
SUSIE COX

Authors' Note:
*Place names are given in their historical context consistent with the quotations
and period cited. Quotations are reproduced verbatim with spellings, names and
punctuation as found in the original.*

CONTENTS

1840

PENINSULAR & ORIENTAL
STEAM NAVIGATION COMPY.

'The absentee who resides in England's colonies — never sees that unpretending piece of bunting of the P. and O. fluttering in the breeze, but it creates a lively emotion in his breast, reminding him of leaving his native land.' Author known by the pseudonym 'A P&O', 1859

I n 1846 a young man, full of excitement and anticipation, having just been offered an engineering job in Java, hurried to the Peninsular and Oriental Steam Navigation Company's office, at 51 St. Mary Axe, in the City of London, to book his passage out. He was anxious, as he had left his booking rather late and knew that the ship would be sailing soon. The P&O booking clerks assured him that there would be a berth for him, but that he would have to buy three separate tickets, which would get him as far as Singapore, the Company's closest port of call to Java.

The first ticket, for the paddle steamer *Oriental*, took him on the start of his journey, from Southampton to Alexandria in Egypt. He would then have to travel overland, across the desert to Suez, where the Company's ship *Precursor* would be waiting to take him on to Point de Galle in Ceylon. From there he would travel aboard *Lady Mary Wood* to Singapore. The very ships' names – *Oriental* and *Precursor* – would have conjured up images to excite.

After having purchased his tickets (which cost £157, including all expenses on board), he went across London to Dent's, in the Strand, to buy a silver pocket chronometer at a cost of thirty guineas. He then returned to his lodgings to collect his luggage, jumped into a hansom cab, and set off for the railway station, near Vauxhall Bridge, to catch the special boat train to Southampton.

On arrival he deposited all his luggage, apart from his carpet bag, at the Peninsular and Oriental Steam Navigation Company's stores, for the Company's regulations demanded that all baggage had to be delivered to their wharf at Southampton docks, the day previous to the steamer's sailing. Having seen to his luggage, he then booked into the Royal Hotel, above the docks, for his overnight stay. Next morning he decided to take a last quick tour of his native Southampton in a cab and arrived at the docks just in time to catch the tug that was ferrying passengers out to his steamer, *Oriental*, which was moored at Hythe, in Southampton Water.

And so began his journey to Singapore, which was to take some forty-six days; other shipping lines, relying on sail rather than steam, would have taken nearer six months. That such an efficiently organised passage was possible, in the mid-nineteenth century, was largely due to the ambition of two men – Brodie McGhie Willcox and Arthur Anderson – the founding fathers of P&O.

In 1848 P&O moved from St. Mary Axe to new offices in Leadenhall Street, opposite the Hon. East India Co., (Engraving, Illustrated London News, *1859)*

'...*I took a cab, and drove all round Kingsland place, St. Mary's, the Ditches, High Street, East Street...round the beach to Northam, up Love Lane to the Asylum ...down the High Street to Southampton Docks...*'

DIARY OF A JAVA-BOUND ENGINEER, 1846

Above: Ticket for a berth in Hindostan, *purchased in 1847 at the P&O office in Calcutta. After serving the Suez to India route for five years,* Hindostan *was returning to Southampton for reconditioning. Opposite: P&O's steamers left Southampton for Alexandria on the 20th of every month carrying passengers, cargo and some 200 bags of letters mostly bound for India. (Henry Fitzcook, c. 1850)*

Arthur Anderson

Brodie McGhie Willcox

Captain Richard Bourne

Sir Thomas Sutherland

First Earl of Inchcape

P&O Coat of Arms, granted in 1937

Second Baron Craigmyle

Sir William Currie

Sir Donald Anderson

Third Earl of Inchcape

Lord Sterling of Plaistow

MEN OF STEAM

The genetic make-up of P&O could best be described as predominately Scottish, for not only were Willcox and Anderson Scots (the latter by birth, the former by descent), but so were the majority of subsequent P&O Chairmen right up to the 1960s. The Scots could well claim that it was their national characteristics of steely determination and adventurous courage – their mettle – that was to build P&O from a modest partnership, chartering ships to run to the Iberian Peninsula in the 1830s, to one of the most extensive and influential shipping companies in the world.

Brodie McGhie Willcox was born to an English father and Scottish mother in Belgium in 1785 and grew up in the North East of England where he described his origins as working class. Willcox had an uncle, a shipbuilder and broker, who may have inspired his nephew's early career as a shipping and insurance broker, in partnership with a Mr N. Carreno in London. Of Carreno little more is known than his name, but that hints at an Iberian connection, and certainly Portugal and Spain were the destinations for the partnership's shipping activities.

In 1815 Willcox and Carreno hired a young clerk Arthur Anderson. Anderson was a Scot through and through, and never forgot his roots. Born into a poor family in the Shetland Islands in 1792 he was known as a 'beach boy', making his living as an unskilled hand in a fish curing business. His employer, Mr. Bolt, was the first to appreciate Anderson's potential, elevating him to a position in the office and encouraging him to join the Navy to further himself. Anderson later recounted that it was Bolt who bade him farewell, as he left to serve as a Captain's clerk in the Navy, urging him to 'do weel and persevere'. The impressionable young Anderson adopted the phrase as his watchword and many years later endowed the Shetland Islands, with a substantial school which still today abides by the motto which so inspired its benefactor.

At the end of the Napoleonic wars Anderson was discharged from the Navy and found himself impoverished and adrift:

'When I first resided in London I was a youth of such slender resources that I was fain to dine upon a pennyworth of cheese and a glass of porter, every other day.'
Arthur Anderson, 1838

His naval experience made him determined to have a career in shipping and an introduction to ship-owner Christopher Hill

'The Peninsular and Oriental Steam Navigation Company is one of the nation's great enterprises. Our name and reputation are of international significance…. Not only am I proud of our name and our history but also profoundly conscious that my appointment as your Chairman comes to me as a privilege and not as a right.'

LORD STERLING, 1983

P&O followed the tradition of commissioning boardroom portraits throughout the Company's history. (For full details refer to Paintings Illustrated on p.248)

led him to Willcox. Within a relatively short time Anderson was making his mark, demonstrating his energy and enthusiasm for business. By 1823 the partnership of Willcox and Carreno became Willcox and Anderson.

During his period in the Navy, Anderson had served in ships sailing around the French and Spanish coasts and was said to be fluent in Spanish – an obvious asset in the Iberian trade. With the departure of Carreno, Willcox and Anderson no longer concerned themselves with insurance, concentrating instead on chartering and owning ships trading not only with the Peninsula but as far afield as Chile and Peru. To begin with, Willcox and Anderson ran ships on an irregular basis, as and when demand arose, but they harboured ambitious plans for 'regular' steam services and they were not alone. In 1834 they published a prospectus for *'a Joint Stock Company, to be called 'THE PENINSULAR STEAM NAVIGATION COMPANY'* and formed of *'a number of the principal Merchants and persons having large interests in the Peninsula'.*

'The plan to be as follows: – To establish a line of Steam Packets, of a large and powerful class, to ply between London, Lisbon and Gibraltar, touching on their outward and homeward passages at Falmouth, Corunna or Vigo, Oporto and Cadiz…It may be mentioned, that it is expected by strict adherence to regularity in the departure, and time on the passage… the British Government will very soon find their advantage, and the advantage of the public, in contracting with the "Peninsular Steam Navigation Company" to carry all the Mails as far as Gibraltar, and vice versa to this country…Such an arrangement would not only be very profitable to the Company, but would in all probability occasion the withdrawal of the present Packet Establishment.'

Peninsular Steam Navigation Company Prospectus, 25th August 1834

Mail was to be their making and it was dear to Anderson's heart. He was psychologically close to his large family but they were geographically scattered and Anderson remembered well the cost and comfort of mail during his time in the Navy:

'Now my dear father's letters of worth inestimable in themselves, being full of wisdom, and counsel and affection, cost me 9d each, or two dinners, or if, as was often the case, he paid the whole postage, they drew upon him too largely.'
Arthur Anderson, 1838

Stamps and marks record the passage of mail from ship to ship and overland. The earliest cover in the P&O collection left Cadiz for London in Iberia, *August 1837.*

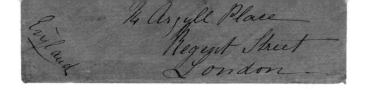

The 'present Packet Establishment', which the Peninsular Steam Navigation Company sought to replace, rested with HM Government whose mail packets, still dependent on sail, could take three weeks to reach Lisbon. In 1823, the Admiralty had assumed responsibility from the Post Office for overseas mail (from Falmouth) and it was to them that the Peninsular Company addressed its first proposal to provide a five-day, steam-powered mail service to the Peninsula in 1836.

A year later the Admiralty invited formal tenders for a Peninsular mail service and, with the help of Captain Richard Bourne RN, it was won by the Company. The Admiralty contract demanded a regular scheduled service of at least one passage a month between Falmouth and the Peninsula ports round to Gibraltar for an annual subsidy of £29,600. Tradition has it that it was the first ocean mail contract of its kind and the date of its signing, 22nd August 1837, has long been regarded as the birth date of P&O.

Carrying the mail was to become the mainstay of P&O, guaranteeing the Company a regular income and shielding it from the vagaries of fluctuations in speculative demand for freight and passengers.

Although Willcox and Anderson's early ambition and intent was clear, Bourne had played a crucial part. Born in Ireland in 1770, Bourne had seen active service in the Navy before and during the Napoleonic wars and, on leaving the service, had traded with his family and associates under the name of the Dublin and London Steam Packet Company, from whom Willcox and Anderson chartered many of their ships. The Bournes were known locally 'as some of the most important men in the country' and enjoyed considerable wealth, operating mail coaches in Ireland. Bourne, the elder and more experienced businessman, understood the potential and the pitfalls of mail contracts and steam navigation.

It was Bourne who brought to Willcox and Anderson the investments necessary for forming a viable company, including the assets of his own company as well as those of the Transatlantic Steam Ship Company. The latter provided P&O with its largest steamers and the expertise of its three directors, Charles Wye Williams, Joseph Ewart and Francis Carleton. Carleton was to be the third Managing Director to sit alongside Willcox and Anderson in the new Company, which was formally incorporated by Royal Charter in 1840.

In the same year P&O won a second mail contract which extended their services to Egypt and included the condition that a regular service between Suez and India be operable

---

Another cover sent in 1854, from China to London, passed between four P&O ships including Pekin *which rescued the mails from* Douro, *wrecked in the China seas.*

'I can assure you…not one is more indebted to parental correspondence than myself. It has conferred on me so much that I would willingly assist to open up the channel and make it less expensive to others. It is certain that where one family goes on to correspond as did ours, a hundred suffer the expense of postage to prevent this most important and delightful intercourse altogether.'

ARTHUR ANDERSON, 1838

Royal Tar *painted in 1838 flying the 'Peninsular' houseflag and* Royal Mail *pennant (Stephen D. Skillett). Overleaf: On longer routes mail schedules were reduced by having a sorting office on board.*

O. STEAMER "PEKIN"

back very handsome +
their teeth they say they die
they fall in love + dont get
me. I cant imagine a girl
so charming. One little
which I got a instead
it only don't frown
tulsheed.

Mr. J. Griffiths Junr.
Bradford Street
Birmingham
England.

England.

On board S.S. Strathaura
Saturday Nov. 17.
the South end of the Red
Sea Mother has told me
Some one has just passed the Twe
leo - The retired nava
says we shall pas

P & O

S.S. Caledonia
3rd May 05.
5 p.m.
Darling Ype. longie '9 did not.
write yesterday - I slept in till the
evening but. I was feeling so stiffy used
that I went down to the cabin
fell asleep + it was but
when I woke up afterw
feeling more like

CALEDONIA

16/5/14

Hawkes.
S. Moldavia.
lles.

INDIA POSTAGE
6 AS

Victoria

of the United Kingdom of Great Britain and Ireland Queen Defender of the
hereinafter named and others have united together for the purpose of establishing
Island of Ceylon China and other places in the East And also for maintaining

Mediterranean Sea and for those purposes have already expended and invested or
propose to open a Subscription for raising a Capital of One Million Pounds Sterling within
Capital our Charter of Incorporation which we are minded to do on the conditions and under
knowledge and mere motion We have given granted constituted and appointed And by these
Joseph Christopher Ewart James Hartley Brodie M.r Gair Willcox Charles ruff williams and
each forwards the capital hereinafter mentioned together with such and so many other persons
time become Proprietors of any part of our Capital shall so long as they shall continue

"The Peninsular and Oriental Steam Navigation Com
and within our Realm or otherwise and shall have continual succession with a Common Sea
purpose of providing Vessels to be impelled by Steam or any other motive power and sha
expedient for establishing communication with our Countries and places as aforesaid or
presents contained shall authorise the said Corporation except for the purpose of communicatin
port or place in the Mediterranean Sea except with our ports or places in Spain and por
public Mails or Dispatches **And further we do hereby direct and**
power or upwards shall be of such construction and strength and their equipments so arra
and that our Vessels so built or used by the said Corporation shall be kept while employe
as aforesaid And that it shall be lawful for the President for the time being of the Boar
the Conveyance of the Public Mails under Contract in order to ascertain if our Vessels
previous Notice given to the Lords Commissioners of our Treasury or the Lord High Tre
made by competent persons one to be named on the part of the said Corporation an
person to be named by the said two Valuers before they proceed to a Valuation **And**
including the amount already expended and invested in acquiring the aforesaid Sh
declare and ordain that the said Corporation shall cause the nam
subscribe or become entitled to any share of the said Capital together with the
to be called the Share Registry Book and that the said Corporation and all persons
established by the said Corporation so that all sales and transfers of and acceptan
do hereby further will and ordain that when and so soon as the

within two years. To mark this new direction the name 'Oriental' was added to the Company's name.

Bourne continued to take an active interest in the new venture but he was advanced in years, and after suffering a stroke in 1850 he died in the following year. An obituary of Bourne, in the *Illustrated London News*, suggested how crucial his initial intervention into the affairs of Willcox and Anderson actually was:

'*...in all human probability the scheme* [of Willcox and Anderson] *would have remained unestablished had not Captain Bourne taken it up. By his skill, energy and means he at once imparted a practical character to what was before only a project.*'
Illustrated London News, 1st November 1851

In 1854 Willcox resigned as Managing Director; although admitting that he could never quite leave the Company, he remained on the board, becoming Chairman in 1858.

'*As the father of the Peninsular Company which became the foundation stone of the Peninsular and Oriental Company, it is impossible for me, so long as I breathe not to take the greatest interest in its prosperity, which I will always promote to the utmost of my power.*'
Brodie McGhie Willcox, 12th June 1854

Although often perceived as a figure in the background, perhaps unfairly overcast by the pushier presence of Anderson, Willcox was a man of some character. A staunch liberal and proponent of free trade, he was twice elected Member of Parliament for Southampton and was a Director of Southampton Docks. He died suddenly in an accident at his home in Essex and a partnership which had endured for forty years came to an abrupt end in 1862; Anderson succeeded Willcox's position as Chairman.

Anderson's health, which had troubled him for many years, was failing and he died in London in 1868. Anderson had remained loyal to his roots throughout. A passionate and proud Shetlander he had served the islands as MP for Orkney and Shetland for one term and addressed the issues which most concerned his birthplace. He established the *Shetland Journal*, set up a Shetland Fishing Company (to open up markets for its fishermen), helped boost the islands' knitting industry, petitioned for crucial lighthouses to be constructed, and brought mail by steamer to his remote island home as early as 1838. His charitable donations to

the islands included building a home for widows in memory of his wife Mary and a secondary school in Lerwick in homage to Mr Bolt.

Willcox and Anderson had lived long enough to see their P&O steamers carrying mail, passengers and cargo all the way east to China and Australia. It must have been more than even they, with the ambition of youth, could have dreamt of.

Anderson's death left James Allan as the sole survivor of the original Company of 1840. Another Scot and a Bourne protégé, Allan, had worked as a clerk in the Dublin and London Steam Packet Company from 1833. He accompanied Bourne to London and became P&O's first Company Secretary in 1840. Allan succeeded Carleton as a Managing Director in 1849 and continued to serve the Company as such until 1872.

'*During this long period Mr. Allan had the entire and well-merited confidence of the Board...it is the duty of the Directors to place on record their high appreciation of his character and attainments and their personal sense of loss which the Company has sustained by his death.*'
P&O Annual Report, 1874

Allan had encouraged another Scot (another Aberdonian) to make the journey south, to take up an appointment as a clerk in P&O at the age of eighteen. It was the start of seventy years of service that was to make Thomas Sutherland one of P&O's most significant Chairmen.

As with Anderson and Willcox, Sutherland was from a poor family, characterising his upbringing as one of 'long graces not long meals.' Sutherland had been in London for only two years before he was sent out, initially to the Company's offices in Bombay and then transferred on to Hong Kong. The switch proved to be the making of him. The Bombay Agency was already well established with room only for 'small fish'. In Hong Kong there was much to be done and Sutherland was quickly able to build up a reputation for himself, both within P&O and within the local community. He set up a company to

P&O's Royal Charter of Incorporation, dated 29th December 1840, enabled the Company to raise £1 million in capital. (Ink on vellum)

The great seal of Queen Victoria (wax)

build the first dock in Hong Kong (laying the foundations for the Hong Kong and Whampoa Dock Company) and in 1864 he established the Hong Kong and Shanghai Banking Corporation, better known today as HSBC.

Sutherland's achievements in Hong Kong did not go unnoticed by Anderson who recalled him to London at the height of P&O's troubles in 1866. Amid rising coal prices, stagnation of trade with the East, and a resultant deficit on the Company's books, the Government served notice on its mail contracts for India and China. Bids were invited from P&O and its competitors including, it was rumoured, the heavily subsidised French line – Messageries Imperiales. P&O already feeling the heat of French competition in the business of carrying cargo, now feared the Company's very existence was at stake. Anderson mustered what power he could for one last battle. In spite of the furore that followed, and was played out publicly in the press, P&O was the only serious contender and its contract terms were passed in Parliament on 29th November 1867.

P&O had done enough to avert one crisis but, as Sutherland was to discover, there was more to come. Before the completion of the Suez Canal in 1869, P&O had no choice but to traverse Egypt by land and to maintain two totally separate fleets to serve routes to and from Alexandria and beyond Suez to India, the Far East and Australia. In addition the Company had made considerable investments and improvements on the overland route that it was reluctant to give up when transit through the Canal became possible. P&O's existing ships were unsuitable for the narrow waterway and, further restricted by the Post Office's reluctance to use the new route, the Company found itself at the mercy of competition on a less than even playing field. It was Sutherland who most fully appreciated the commercial and political implications of the Suez Canal.

By 1872 Sutherland had joined Allan as the one of P&O's Managing Directors and, in less than a decade, he became the Company's youngest ever Chairman at the age of forty-seven. Once in the Chair, Sutherland, with an enviable command of French, negotiated successfully with the De Lesseps family, to ensure much improved access to the Suez Canal at commercially viable rates for both P&O and British ship-owners generally. The so called 'London Programme' was agreed in P&O's office and gave Britain a voice in the running of the Canal.

Addressing the need for new ships, Sutherland ordered four 'Jubilee' liners – *Victoria*, *Britannia*, *Oceana* and *Arcadia* – two of which were built at Greenock, Sutherland's

Thomas Sutherland in the Hong Kong office (seated right of Max Fisher, P&O's Superintendent) c.1859

'He brought the company out of what might be described as a "slough of despond" and by his energy and ability he left it a sound and prosperous concern.'

LORD INCHCAPE, 8TH DECEMBER 1915

'P. and O.' a caricature of Thomas Sutherland by Carlo Pellegrini 'Ape' published in Vanity Fair *on 22nd August 1887, for P&O's Jubilee*

In 1844 the Company acquired the lease for a plot of land, known as 'Marine Lot 16', in the west part of Victoria in Hong Kong and built a substantial property marked on the waterfront by a flag pole and small wooden jetty. (Marciano Antonio Baptista)

parliamentary constituency. From the outset P&O's management thought it essential to have its interests represented in Parliament, and the 'liberal' lineage of Willcox and Anderson was continued by Sutherland who became a Liberal MP in 1884.

In 1915, after presiding over the longest reign at the top, almost thirty-four years, Sutherland was weary, admitting that: *'I have been riding at single anchor and ready to hoist my Blue Peter at the shortest notice'*. He had been waiting for the right man, but it took a merger in 1914 to provide a suitable successor in yet another Scot, James Lyle Mackay, later the first Earl of Inchcape. Inchcape was the first to pay tribute to his predecessor as 'a great Victorian' who had raised the Company *'phoenix-like, from near disaster to a new dominating position'*:

'Sir Thomas Sutherland will surely go down as one of the great Victorians. No individual of his time did more to create and maintain the supremacy of British shipping and the high regard in which British shipowners and their methods were and are held among foreign competitors.'
Lord Inchcape, 7th January 1922

The son of a Captain, Inchcape, was born into shipping in the Scottish town of Arbroath. Like his predecessors at P&O he moved to London working for a time as a clerk in a shipping agency. In 1874 he began his lifelong association with India joining Mackinnon, Mackenzie & Co. in Calcutta. The partnership of another two Scots, William Mackinnon and Robert Mackenzie, had begun in Calcutta in 1847. By 1856 'Mackinnons' had founded the British India Steam Navigation Company (BI) and, as shipping agents, the company served both BI and P&O.

Like Sutherland, Inchcape's rise through the ranks was meteoric. At just twenty-six he had become a partner in Mackinnons and in India he was building a considerable reputation not only in the shipping world but in the colony itself. With the death of Sir William Mackinnon in 1893, Inchcape was called back to London to run BI's office there. His time in India had served him well. Inchcape had gained respect and public recognition at the highest levels earning him great plaudits and, in time, a peerage in 1911.

From 1903 Inchcape and Sutherland had sat on the Suez Canal Company board together, representing the interests of their respective lines. The two men knew and liked each other well and when Inchcape was appointed BI's Chairman in 1913, they masterminded the historic merger of P&O

Victoria, first of the 'Jubilee' class, was launched in 1887. The new steamers could reach India in sixteen days and Australia in thirty-five. (R. H. Neville-Cumming)

Above: Oceana, *the third 'Jubilee', was built in Belfast at the Harland and Wolff yard and made her maiden voyage to Australia in 1888. (Anglo-chinese School)*

Below: Arcadia *was the sister ship to* Oceana *built at the same yard in just over a year. (Gerald Maurice Burn)*

and BI in utter secrecy. Following the union in 1914, all P&O Directors became Directors of BI, and vice versa, in a board arrangement which lasted until 1957. In all other respects the two companies continued to run separately, complementing each others' services and routes.

Once established in the 'chair', Inchcape took a very firm grip of the reins, remaining virtually unchallengeable for the next seventeen years. Admired for his aggressively clever programme of acquisitions, both during and immediately after the First World War, Inchcape ensured that the P&O group fleet was larger at the end of the war than at its start, in spite of the Company's war losses.

Between 1916 and 1923, P&O's acquisitions included the New Zealand Shipping Company, Federal Steam Navigation Company, Union Steamship Company of New Zealand, Hain Steamship Company, James Nourse Ltd., Strick Line, General Steam Navigation Company, Khedivial Mail Line and a majority share in the Orient Line. The size of the combined fleet had more than doubled, numbering some 500 vessels, making P&O, for a time, the largest shipping company in the world.

Inchcape not only reigned supreme within P&O but had become the doyen of British shipping, sitting on numerous related government committees and holding key posts within the industry. Inchcape had presided over P&O's transformation from a shipping line to a worldwide shipping group and hinted at its future diversification with an interest in the P&O Banking Corporation, which was set up in 1920.

Inchcape died suddenly on 23rd May 1932 in Monaco, his biographer recounting that even on that last day: *'the daily mail-bag still arrived from Leadenhall Street: the affairs of the company were still tightly clenched in his hands'.*
Hector Bolitho, 1936

Although in his time all seemed well, P&O's fleet being considerable in number, its investors receiving large dividends, and Inchcape himself continually in the limelight, the Company's balance sheet told a different story. A later biographer critiquing his contribution wrote:

'Inchcape's decisions were not always in the best interests of the long-term future of P&O, he failed to confront the problems faced by British shipping as a whole in inter-war years.'
Stephanie Jones, 1989

By his extrovert personality, combining a bluff humour and tremendous energy, Inchcape was able to keep up what

Inchcape's acquisition of a number of existing shipping lines ensured P&O's position as the largest shipping company in the world. (Ogden's Cigarette cards, 1906)

'I mean to slip away next month in a P. & O. steamer, the most comfortable place in the world to be in, to spend a few weeks in the Sunny South, not to do any work, but to play deck quoits and, at intervals, if the Captain will permit me, to go on the bridge, or to recline in a long deck chair....'

LORD INCHCAPE, 12TH DECEMBER 1923

In 1931 Inchcape (centre right) joined Captain Cecil Brooks (centre left) and the crew of Ranpura, *taking part in the Royal Naval Review at Spithead.*

appeared a successful front, leaving underlying problems and hidden accounting files to his successor and son-in-law.

The Rt Hon Alexander Shaw, (later 2nd Baron Craigmyle) had married Inchcape's eldest daughter, Lady Margaret Cargil Mackay in 1913. By the time Shaw succeeded Inchcape, he had been a Director of P&O since 1920 and had twice served as Liberal MP for the Scottish constituency of Kilmarnock Burghs. He held numerous directorships in banking and shipping and was well equipped to face the challenges ahead:

'We are passing through very difficult times, when we have to meet not only the collapse of world trade but the competition of heavily subsidised foreign lines…My firm belief is that if we continue to march shoulder to shoulder we shall keep our flag flying on the seven seas.'
The Rt Hon Alexander Shaw, 8th June 1932

Shaw quickly recruited Sir William Currie as his Deputy Chairman and Managing Director in 1932. Currie shared Inchcapes's lifelong attachment to India. Born in Calcutta, educated in Scotland and Cambridge, Currie qualified as a chartered accountant in Glasgow. Returning to Calcutta in 1910, he joined his father at Mackinnons. Currie was influential in India, gathering a string of appointments and honours: Sheriff of Calcutta, President of the Bengal Chamber of Commerce, Member of the Legislative Council and Member of the Council of State and receiving a knighthood for his services there in 1925. Like his father, he rose to senior partner in Mackinnons before transferring to London in 1926.

On the eve of the Second World War, in 1938, Currie became P&O's Chairman, a position he was to hold until 1960. It was Currie who was faced with the difficult task of managing the Company in wartime whilst looking after Britain's wider interests, having been appointed Director of the Liner Division of the Ministry of Transport in 1942. Like Inchcape in the First World War, Currie was on the one hand overseeing the conversion of his own requisitioned fleet and, on the other, helping to plan the Allies' strategies for the invasion of North Africa, Sicily and Normandy. Closer to home Currie set up emergency headquarters for the Company at Croxley Green in Hertfordshire. During the war the P&O group was to lose just under half its fleet and almost 1,000 employees.

As Chairman throughout the 1950s, Currie not only had to rebuild a depleted fleet, but to face up to a post-war

Calcutta was home to Mackinnon Mackenzie & Co. and BI and it was here that the first Earl of Inchcape and Currie began their illustrious careers. (Photo c. 1930s)

'The demise of the First Earl was expected…. But his death, when it came, shook the shipping world and his own kingdoms, both of which he had dominated. What had not been anticipated was something which electrified his minions throughout Mackinnon Mackenzie. When, in due course, the contents of the will were declared, it emerged that he had provided for every assistant in the firm to receive a month's salary and each of his partners £1,000.'

SIR ANDREW CRICHTON, 1986

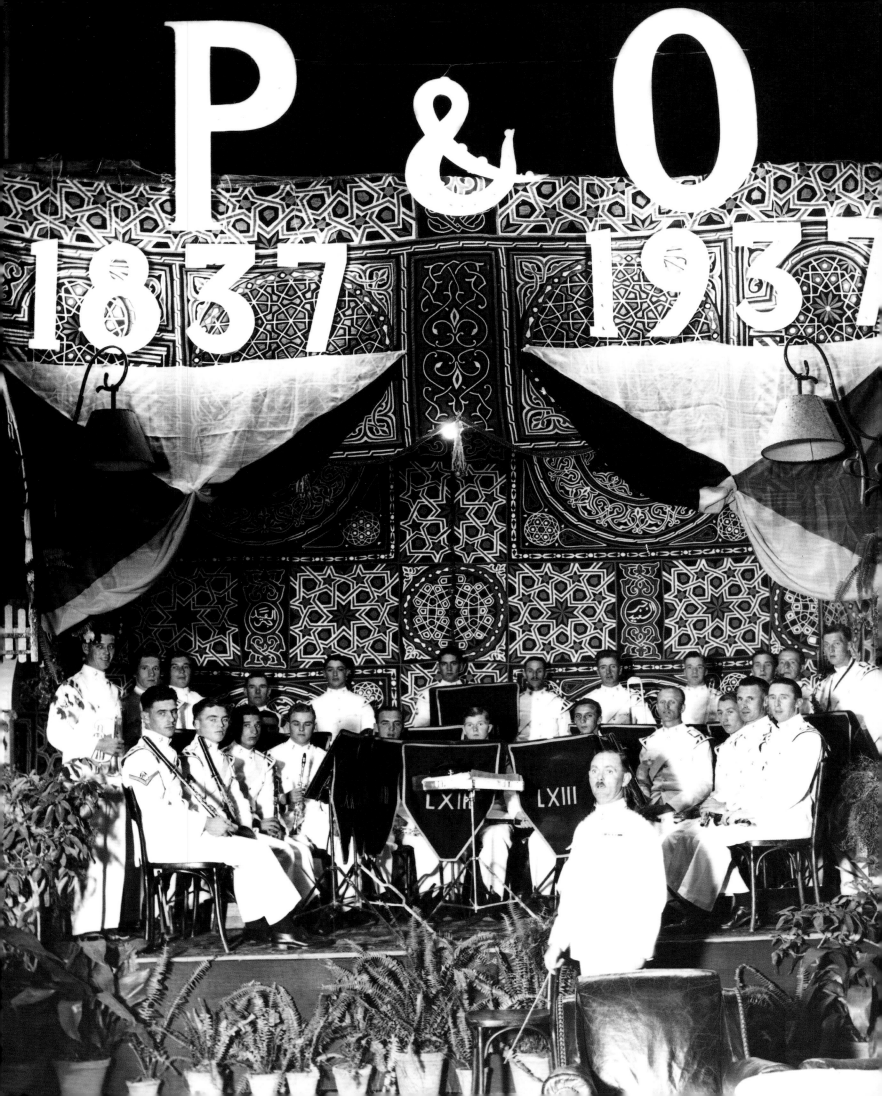

'*One hundred years of P&O. What enterprise, what heroism, what determination, and what romantic thoughts spring to mind at the sound of that famous name! Spain, the Peninsula, India and the Orient – what victory over difficulties!*'

RT. REVEREND G. VERNON SMITH,
14TH OCTOBER 1937

The Company's centenary was celebrated with concerts, dinners and services both on board the fleet and ashore in P&O's principal bases including Aden, which was elaborately decorated for the occasion.

world with dramatically changing transport needs. The prospect of commercial air transport was emerging as a threat to the future of shipping in general. In P&O's traditional territories there was a growing wave of independence starting with India in 1947 and cascading across the British Empire to the Far East. Each nation was eager to assert its right to own and operate its own shipping lines.

The decade brought with it the communist victory in China, affecting trade with Hong Kong, along with the rapid rebuilding of Japan as a competitive trading nation. The Suez Crisis of 1956 was an added disturbance to trade, the canal being the keystone to P&O's operations. Currie was becoming increasingly pessimistic and exhausted:

'…as he grew older, slower, and less able to make swift decisions his juniors believed essential, so it became more difficult for anyone to point out that he really ought to retire.'
David and Stephen Howarth, 1986

Nevertheless it was Currie who saw the Company's last passenger liner – *Canberra* – through to her launch in 1960 and with this achieved, he stepped down at the age of seventy-six. In his twenty-two years at the helm he was known affectionately as Sir Willy and was genuinely loved in the Company and esteemed in the shipping industry at large.

In a well-worn path, another Scot of shipping stock, Sir Donald Anderson, succeeded Currie as Chairman. Anderson's family firm, Anderson, Green & Co. ran the Orient Line, but Anderson himself had moved into P&O in the 1930s and had been Currie's deputy since 1950. P&O's acquisition of the remaining shares in the Orient Line, in 1960, integrated the two companies completely and brought the Anderson family back together in one firm.

Anderson was all too aware of the challenges that now faced P&O, not least the excess of worldwide shipping capacity and the rise in the number of vessels running under flags of convenience, with all their financial advantages. He was both clear sighted and courageous, cutting costs and rationalising where possible, and turning P&O's focus on to more profitable areas of growth in tankers, bulk carriers and containers. It was Anderson who was instrumental in combining with other leading British liner shipping companies to form Overseas Containers Ltd., (OCL) and although this attracted crippling union opposition in the short term, in the longer term it was to be where P&O's future lay. For this alone Anderson has justly been called the outstanding shipping man of his generation.

In 1971 Anderson retired leaving his second cousin, and former Orient Line Director, Ford Irvine Geddes in the Chair. Excepting his wartime stint at the Ministry of War Transport, Anderson had served P&O for thirty-two years. In contrast Geddes' chairmanship was to last for only just over a year and ended in controversy.

A wholesale restructuring of the Company had begun under Anderson, but a major proposal for diversification into construction – that P&O should make a bid for the Bovis company – was, at that time, a step too far. After an embittered and very public controversy, P&O shareholders rejected the Bovis deal in 1972. Geddes was replaced by the third Earl of Inchcape, Kenneth James William Mackay, who had been actively opposed to the purchase of Bovis. Forty years after his grandfather had held the same post, the third Earl was to move P&O forwards into a very different seascape where the Empire and mail contracts were long gone and line voyages were soon to disappear. Fortunately, Inchcape saw the reality of the situation rather more courageously than some of his forebears:

'A business must be able to contract as well as expand, and to change its shape in a changing world.'
Lord Inchcape, 2nd May 1979

In a fitting twist it was Inchcape who in 1974 presided over P&O's acquisition of Bovis for one-fifth of the valuation placed on it two years earlier. Diversification for P&O was inevitable, but only at the right price.

Inchcape retired in 1983 and was succeeded by Jeffrey Maurice Sterling, later Lord Sterling. It was the Chairman of OCL, Sir Andrew Crichton, who had first spotted Sterling and proposed his appointment to the P&O Board in 1980. As a barometer of the changing times, Sterling was a 'finance and property', rather than a 'shipping', man and just what the now diversified P&O needed. His first challenge

*From 1883, P&O shared the Australia mail contract with the Orient Line, operating
alternately to deliver a fortnightly service. (Poster by Abram Games, 1951)*

was to repel a hostile bid from Trafalgar House Investments, a major city conglomerate. Sterling's reputation in the City and smart handling of the situation earned him respect and the chairmanship. The merger with his own company, Sterling Guarantee Trust, gave P&O a firm foothold in property to shore up its defences against future challenges. Ably aided by Sir Bruce MacPhail, Sterling's emphasis on profitability, although obliging the P&O Group to break with much of its traditional shipping past, kept it afloat.

Although not a Scot, a Liberal or a shipping man, Sterling's passion for P&O matched his predecessors. He took enormous pride in celebrating P&O's 150th Anniversary in 1987. As a lasting legacy, the Company financed the restoration of the house of Arthur Anderson's birth, 'Böd of Gremista', from where he would have been proud to see the Peninsular flag flying on P&O Scottish Ferries plying the waters between the Shetland Islands and the mainland.

Over 150 years P&O had become a very different and diverse Company. As Sterling acknowledged in 1995, the Group had interests far beyond shipping:

'We have always paid the highest attention to the needs of our passengers – but not just passengers. We can carry your goods around the world, from door to door, by ship or barge or truck or train. We can take you and your family and your car on holiday and sell you a good dinner and duty frees in the process. We can fuel your power stations and feed your steel mills. We can develop and operate your ports.

Away from the sea, we can build your home and hotels and airports. We can rent you a warehouse or an office block or a shop, stage your exhibitions or your conferences or your pop concerts. We can store your frozen foods and clean your offices and feed your employees.

All these are services to our worldwide customers for we are a worldwide company. But we are a British company too.'
Lord Sterling, 1995

A decade later Sterling retired. Addressing the Company's shareholders for the last time, he reflected on the 'rare privilege' of being a Chairman of P&O:

'From the P&O bridge I have set course in choppy weather and calm waters, I have dropped anchor or cast off or steered courses in all sorts of directions. I have been thrown lifelines and life belts – and I have been asked to walk the plank. I have also floated some businesses, but that's something different. Now I shall be floating away myself.'
Lord Sterling, 13th May 2004

Sterling was succeeded in 2004 by Sir John Parker as Non-Executive Chairman and Robert Woods as Chief Executive Officer. By this time, P&O had divested, reinvested and refocused its efforts in three key directions: ferries, logistics, and ports. In so doing it had become one of the largest port operators in the world. It was this that attracted the Dubai port operator, DP World, which purchased The Peninsular and Oriental Steam Navigation Company in 2006.

Opposite: A full-size replica William Fawcett *(traditionally regarded as P&O's first ship) moored at the Royal Naval College, Greenwich as the centrepiece of the 150th Anniversary spectacular.*

Above: Böd of Gremista, Arthur Anderson's birthplace in the Shetland Islands, viewed from the bow of a P&O Scottish ferry.

HOME PORTS

From 1688 the port of Falmouth in Cornwall was the mail packet station for the Mediterranean fleets and was principal port of departure for P&O's earliest mail services, although the Company's ships were based in London. On the first Iberian mail contract sailing in 1837, the P&O paddle-steamer *Don Juan* left London on 1st September and Falmouth three days later on 4th September.

In 1840 the Admiralty announced that Southampton would replace Falmouth for the carriage of mail. In the same year P&O's *Oriental* left Southampton on the first Egyptian mail sailing and the Company began to establish its base in the town. P&O set about negotiating rates with the Southampton Railway Company, for freight and passenger services to and from London, and purchasing offices. As new docks were still under construction the Company had to anchor its ships offshore and to ferry passengers and freight to and fro in small tugs. In 1842, *Liverpool*, *Tagus*, and *Hindostan* all sailed from the 'outer dock', and the *Chusan* made her historic departure for Australia from Southampton, in 1852, when a further extension to the Mail contract had been agreed.

'She went off in gallant style, and under ordinary circumstances there is no doubt but that she will make a rapid and successful passage. A few of the directors, with several noblemen and gentlemen interested in the prosperity of the Australian colonies, assembled on board at Southampton, and accompanied the ship on her first voyage as far as Calshot Castle.'
Illustrated London News, 22nd May 1852

Opposite: *Southampton docks in 1889 viewed from the water tower of No. 3 Dry Dock. P&O's history with Southampton dates back to 1840 when the Company's first Agent in the town was Thomas Hill, Arthur Anderson's brother-in-law.*

For some thirty years, Southampton remained P&O's home port. The Company not only owned offices, wharves and warehouses, but a complete colony of homes for its employees and their families. There was also a large laundry, operated by widows of employees, for washing and repairing the fleet's linen. By the 1850s over 2,000 people, connected with P&O, were resident there and a school for employees' children had been set up.

Southampton was also the parliamentary constituency of Willcox, a seat which he held there from 1847. Strategic advantages aside, Willcox was an active and popular representative of the city. The announcement of his death in 1862: *'excited much regret among all classes of inhabitants. Flags are hoisted to-day at half mast on all the shipping in the docks and in several parts of the town and many of the tradesmen have their shutters up as a mark of respect to the memory of the late member'.*
The Times, 8th November 1862

It was, another Chairman, Sutherland, who presided over the return of P&O's main port to London, first announced in 1874. The news came as a considerable blow to the town but Sutherland saw the move as an essential economy. Although well positioned for mail and passengers (reaching the port by rail), Southampton was unpopular with shippers and merchants most of whom were located in London and resented the extra carriage expense of shipping goods up and down to Southampton.

Sutherland understood the increasing importance of freight to the Company's income and was alert to shippers' threats to take their business elsewhere. As a result, the Royal Docks became P&O's cargo base in the Port of London, and Tilbury its main passenger terminus. The Company had a full complement of staff at Tilbury, dealing with arrivals and departures, loading and discharging, inspection and maintenance. As late as the 1950s there were still some sixty employees at the port – planning the berths, arranging the necessary tugs and pilots, and positioning the stevedores for loading, unloading and cleaning the holds. A purser was always on hand for provisioning, and unloading large quantities of empty bottles.

Although schedules were set and port berths booked months in advance, it was not until P&O ships were well on their way home – 'a China ship clear of Port Said or an Australian ship clear of Marseilles' – that the Company's agents could confidently cable Tilbury with an estimated time of arrival. With different tugs and pilots required

In 1957 P&O Dock Superintendent, Captain Hand, and his staff moved to a new office at the Royal Docks previously used by the Port of London Authority.

'*The* Pekin *anchored off Gravesend and Tilbury about 6.30, the customs house officers came aboard and the cabin luggage of the people who intended getting off examined, and then we got into the tender boat alongside, and steamed to the railway station having just taken tickets to Fenchurch Street.*'

HELEN FORD, *PEKIN*, 1888

Ceylon *anchored in the Thames at Tilbury in 1895. With the last of the passengers arriving by steam tender, the ship flies the Blue Peter signalling readiness to leave. (R. H. Neville-Cumming)*

for sea, river and dock, precise instructions were wired to in-coming vessels setting in motion a well-oiled chain of events in a tight turnaround masterminded by the Tilbury shore staff:

'*Endeavour to arrive Brixham Noon, Gravesend 07.00 and Anchor. Alongside Stage 09.00. Passengers disembark 11.00 onwards, Special trains about Noon, 13.00, 13.45 arriving St.Pancras one hour later Stop. Leave Landing Stage for No.33 berth Tilbury Dock 14.00 Stop. How many aliens landing?*'
Captain G. Bridge, 1952

Further upstream, the Royal Docks were home to more P&O staff and ships. A wooden dock office was built for P&O's Branch Service to Australia to coincide with the opening of King George V Dock in 1921. The office sufficed for many years until the Dock Superintendent and his staff took up residence in a comparatively sturdy, brick building in 1957.

Although the Company continued to use London as its home port, P&O ships did use Southampton, on occasion, the local press announcing emotionally in 1893:

'*The old P&O flag was once more flying from the masthead of the P&O offices in Canute Rd yesterday, a sight which has not been seen in the port since 1881.*'
The Southampton Times, 25th February 1893.

The celebrations were somewhat premature, but sightings of P&O ships in the port did increase, particularly so in times of war. As P&O's mail steamers were some of the largest and fastest ships afloat, the requisition of the Company's tonnage to carry troops for the Government was part and parcel of the mail contract. The first major call on the fleet came with the Crimean War when eleven ships departed with their troops from Southampton. Similarly, in the Boer War, the two World Wars and even the Falklands War, P&O ships sailed on their national duty from Southampton.

In the inter-war years, when P&O ships were increasingly being used for off-peak cruising, Southampton was the preferred choice, saving passengers the additional sailing day to and from London. P&O's last passenger liners, *Oriana* and *Canberra*, were too large for Tilbury, and in 1969 Southampton became once more P&O's home port for passenger operations (until the last line voyage sailed in 1973) and cruising.

On 10th October 1969 Himalaya *became the last P&O passenger liner to depart from Tilbury. A special luncheon on board marked the historic occasion. (William Eric Thorp)*

HEAD OFFICE

Willcox and Anderson first operated from 46 Lime Street in the heart of the City of London before moving a short distance to rented premises at 51 St. Mary Axe in 1836. By the mid 1840s P&O's rapid growth demanded more administrative space and the Managing Directors acquired the King's Arms coaching inn and hotel in nearby Leadenhall Street. The architect Samuel Beachcroft was commissioned to design the Company's first head office, in a Greek Doric revival style, at a cost of £8,000. The new building was completed in two years and in 1848 P&O moved to 122 Leadenhall Street. Perfectly positioned in the hub of the London's shipping district, and not too far from the Thames, Leadenhall Street was to remain the heart of Company's business for over a century.

By 1859 an impressive three-storey stone building, surmounted appropriately by a sculpture of Neptune, had been added. The Company's new building faced on to Leadenhall Street and had been designed by the architect Henry Currey. As well as additional offices, it boasted a dining room for the Directors and a subterranean bullion chamber with 'a place for raising and lowering the precious metal by hydraulic means'. A sizeable courtyard separated the new building from Beachcroft's original, providing a turning circle for the Director's carriages as they arrived for their weekly meetings.

Bit by bit, over the years, adjacent properties were bought up so that, by the end of the century, a conglomerate of buildings resembling a rabbit warren existed. A young clerk recalled:

'I soon learned my way about the labyrinthine corridors and stairways of the building, plotting the best course to the different departments, outward bound via the cash stairs and homewards by the way of the management floor, or the lift on the St. Mary Axe entrance and the freight department'.
Olaf Buggé reminiscing in 1979

The top floor was where the Chairman, Directors and Senior Managers were housed. Between it and the ground floors the space was divided geographically, relating to P&O's areas of operation – India/Pakistan/Ceylon, the Straits/Hong Kong/Japan, and Australia. Here the operational managers dealt with the job of filling the fleet's capacity together with the commissioning, decommissioning, maintenance and manning of the fleet and all matters concerning the movement of mail and freight.

An elegant courtyard linked the Leadenhall Street frontage of '122' to the earliest P&O offices. The outline of the circular bullion lift can be seen to the right of the photograph.

The bullion lift in the middle of the courtyard remained in use well into the 1920s. Precious cargo was a lucrative trade for P&O and it was quite an ordinary sight to see shining ingots of silver being loaded to and from horse-drawn carriages.

From the very beginning Leadenhall Street not only served as Head Office but as booking office as well. Would-be passengers were invited there to sample the Company's exceptional wines that they would be served on board, if they decided to travel P&O. They could also see the exact position of the berth they were booking:

'The Managers have adopted a plan of having at the Chief Office complete models of the Cabins, by which a Passenger may see at once the size and situation of any cabin or bed-place as well as if he were on board ship – a facility that engraved plans cannot give.'
John Nicholson, 1932

'I am a personal friend of one of your Directors but I don't want to trouble him. Of course if you cannot give me a cabin de luxe on the port side of the Strathpiffle, mid-October, I shall have to write to him.'

ABOUT OURSELVES, DECEMBER 1952

Besides tickets and berths the booking office of Leadenhall Street catered for freight services and passengers wishing to ship cars and personal effects.

By 1874 P&O had opened an office at 25 Cockspur Street, by Trafalgar Square, which served as the West End passenger booking and luggage operation (in addition to that being run on the ground floor in Leadenhall Street). In 1899 this was replaced with larger premises acquired in nearby Northumberland Avenue. When the opportunity arose in 1918, P&O returned to Cockspur Street purchasing nos 14-16, a splendidly sculpture-festooned building built for a German bank and remodelled by Arthur T. Bolton for the Hamburg America Line in 1906-8. At the outbreak of the First World War, it was requisitioned by the Government and then retained as part of German reparations. It was something of a coup for P&O, who quickly set about making the grand building its own, replacing the existing decoration with an enormous relief by the sculptor Ernest Gillick featuring two bronze caryatids representing the Orient on the left and Britannia on the right (accompanied by putti holding a lotus flower and the trident); the whole symbolised P&O's domination of the seas from Britain to China. Above the entrance Gillick placed the 'rising sun' and the Company motto: 'Quis Separabit' ('who will separate us').

In the 1920s Cockspur Street was alive with shipping, rail companies and travel agents competing for custom. Striking window displays, which changed every few months, were used to entice would-be passengers and delight the casual passerby. Inside the office the days immediately before the Friday weekly sailings were particularly hectic, the basement baggage rooms bulging with passengers' trunks and suitcases to be transferred to Tilbury or Royal Docks. The responsibility for filling berths, and processing P&O passengers from booking to departing, occupied one of the largest departments in the Company and was presided over by the Passenger Manager:

'Nobody whose family tree has not in the dim and distant past included some remote connection to Job, Machiavelli, Baron Munchausen and David Garrick can ever aspire to reach that lonely pinnacle upon which sits the Passenger Manager.'
About Ourselves, 1952

Cockspur Street remained the Company's main and most elegant Passage Department until the 1970s and the demise of line voyages.

'Titled persons, viceroys, pro-consuls, Governors, Maharajahs, merchant princes, dowagers, missionaries, planters, and such like – a cross section of Empire – would always travel by P&O;

'I joined the P&O company when I was a lad of eighteen in 1905. In those days considerable influence was required before one could enter its portals as an employee. The influence I had was my father, who was superintendent engineer of the branch line ex Lund Line. I was not particularly anxious to join, as I was quite happy with a firm of tea brokers, but to my father there was no better place next to heaven, than in the fold of the P&O Co.'

ASHLEY RANDALL, REMINISCING IN AUGUST 1973

Poised between Canadian Pacific Railways and Thomas Cook on Cockspur Street, was P&O House, decorated in 1937 for the Company's centenary and the coronation of King George VI.

*that imposing office and all it stood for seemed as immutable and
fixed as the stars in their courses. It was inconceivable that in the
forseeable future it would cease to function as a passenger office'.*
Olaf Buggé reminiscing in 1973

In the City, Leadenhall Street had continued to expand.
In 1893 a new building, No. 128 (adjacent to 122), was
completed to the design of Thomas Collcutt. The acquisition
of several shipping lines during the First World War and
the creation of the P&O Banking Corporation called
for another building, which was completed by Collcutt's
successors, Collcutt and Hamp, in 1926, on the corner of
Leadenhall Street and St. Mary Axe.

Few could fail to be impressed by Leadenhall Street with
its great courtyard and the imposing boardroom where the
Company held its annual meetings of shareholders. With the
first Earl of Inchcape in the Chair it was a dapper affair:

*'The AGMs were great occasions. The Chairman wore morning clothes,
white slips under the waistcoat, stiff cuffs, white spats, the lot.'*
Sir Andrew Crichton, reminiscing in 1986

Leadenhall Street remained at the heart of British
shipping and the P&O Company for the best part of 130
years. But the City streets were changing. The patchwork
of buildings that had served the Company for so long was
demolished in 1964. Before the bulldozers began, a former
purser paid his respects to '122' where he had started his
P&O career in 1905:

*'As I went from that empty building, to the astonishment of
passers-by who may have seen me, I turned and raised my hat
in reverence to it. I had spent one or two happy years within its
portals, and under its aegis developed from a callow youth to
a middle aged man'.*
Ashley Randall, writing in 1973

The new concrete P&O building, which towered over
the site of the old (in 1969), belonged to a very different age.
Like the Company itself, the building reflected the need for
modernity and the flexibility to adapt quickly to changing
commercial conditions. In 1984 P&O cut its last ties with
Leadenhall Street for a new mooring in the 'property' heart
of the West End. 79 Pall Mall was home to P&O's Head
Office for twenty years before the Company moved to a new
building in Palace Street aptly described as a modern space
resounding with P&O history.

---

*Window displays were a feature of Cockspur Street. The Polish artist, Zygmunt Kowalewski,
created this striking montage using the latest plastics available. (John Jochimsen, 1971)*

'*Where once many of these reminders of Britain's heritage could be seen in the P&O's former imposing headquarters in Pall Mall, they are now to be found in the nearby ultra-modern premises of DP World, where staff have the privilege of some of the magnificent paintings adorning their office walls and splendid maritime artefacts in glass showcases between their desks.*'

LLOYD'S LIST, 2011

Above: Ship models are an important part of the award-winning heritage displays at Palace Street. (Briony Campbell) Opposite: Detail of a 1:48 scale model of Syria *dating from 1901. (David Morris)*

POST CARD

Steamer Point. Aden.

View from Clock Tower, Bombay

Port Said. Entrance of the Suez Canal

Victoria Jetty, Penang.

The Mail Wharf, Fremantle, W.A.

Steamer Point. The Inner Harbour and Landing Pier. Aden.

'Every Britisher and Imperialist is proud of the Peninsular and Oriental Navigation Company. We feel it is part of the British Constitution. You can only realise this by imagining what would happen if the whole fleet were to disappear tomorrow.' J. Henniker Heaton, *Medina*, December 1913

The Company was not just identified with the Empire that it served, it was frequently confused with the British Empire itself, at least that part which lay east of Suez. From the first mail contract in 1837 to the last, P&O played the part of the Empire's postman and sometime envoy.

Overseas commerce and government were so inextricably intertwined that the relationship between P&O and the British Government overseas became a mutual one. Not only was P&O able to establish depots in nascent colonies, but often Company employees would take an active part in the development and governance of these colonies. The fortunes of P&O reflected, to a considerable extent, the waxing and waning of British imperial power.

Gerald Graham wrote of the British Empire after the Battle of Waterloo:

'Fortified with bases on every significant trade route and practically immune from serious competition Britain, for the first and only time, stood in comfortable "splendid isolation".'
Gerald Graham

P&O was perfectly positioned to take full advantage of this power base, quickly following the trade opportunities that opened up on the Empire mail routes.

MEDITERRANEAN MAILS

Gibraltar was the gateway to the Mediterranean and with the extension of P&O's mail contract to Egypt it became a significant port of call for mail and passengers. The Company's first agent in Gibraltar was William Smith, who had previously been an agent for Bourne's Dublin and London Steam Packet Company. The agency continued in the hands of the Smith family (later joined by the Imossi family) for over 120 years.

Heavily fortified, Gibraltar was a strategic asset for the British:

'As the ship was steaming into the bay we had a good view of the fortifications, dockyard etc. guns peeping out of all sorts of impossible places at a tremendous height. It reminded me altogether of a giant's castle in a fairy tale.'
F. R. Kendall, 17th February 1858

Malta provided P&O with another strategic base, positioned as an intermediate port of call between Gibraltar and Alexandria. It was also conveniently located for the mail ports of Marseilles and Brindisi to the north and Constantinople in the east. As the Peninsular Steam Navigation Company, P&O first sailed to Malta in 1836 for

The Company's mail steamers not only conveyed postcards but were frequently the subject of them. Today the P&O collection numbers over 2,500 historic postcards.

'We skirted along the dark, savage mountains of the African coast, and came to the Rock just before gunfire. It is the very image of an enormous lion, crouched between the Atlantic and the Mediterranean and set there to guard the passage for its British mistress...'

WILLIAM MAKEPEACE THACKERAY, 1846

Above: Gibraltar from a Company steamer in 1846. Early calls were limited by the mail contract to just six hours and timed with connecting mails. (Andrew Nicholl)

Opposite: Gibraltar viewed over a century later from Arcadia in 1960.

the curious purpose of collecting four giraffes bound for the Zoological Society in London.

A new P&O mail contract in 1853 linked Malta to Marseilles for the express mails. With this service the Company could offer passengers a faster, alternative route to Alexandria avoiding the notorious Bay of Biscay. In time passengers could enjoy the 'P&O Overland Express' – one of the 'most luxurious trains in operation on the Continent' – for the journey through France. By the 1930s the weekly service from Victoria Station in London to the quayside at Marseilles took just twenty-two hours. In those days the 'chef du train', known simply as Napoleon: *'knew and recognized most of the regular P&O passengers, who for reasons of time, convenience or simply a dread of the Bay, preferred to travel by this route'*.

For mail officers Friday at Marseilles meant only one thing – loading mail. Consignments of European mails arrived on the quayside during the day to be joined late at night with the arrival of the British mails. Each bag of mail was inspected, counted, loaded into a sling and hoisted aboard. The quantities were staggering: in 1910, 25,000 tons of mail were shipped from London, Marseilles and Brindisi on P&O ships alone.

In 1870 the Company began a weekly service between the other major Mediterranean mail port, Brindisi, and Alexandria in response to the Franco-Prussian war which diverted the mails from the normal route through France.

'No doubt this is the most wonderful sight of the voyage…. An interminable procession of bulky mail bags, laden with letters from every part of the world, files its way from the quay to the hold, each bag carefully checked by the officer whose duty it is to fulfil this responsible office. It comes to one as a startling surprise that there can possibly be so many letters travelling about the world, and when one realises that this same scene is enacted every week throughout the year it becomes an occasion for even still greater wonder.'
Harry Furniss at Brindisi, 1898

P&O established an elegant agent's office on the quayside at Brindisi and won an Italian contract to run a cargo and passenger service between Venice, Ancona, Brindisi and Egypt, which ran until 1900. P&O's express steamers continued the Brindisi link to Alexandria right up to the First World War, after which Marseilles resumed its role as the Company's connection to the rail service across Europe.

Mail bags piled up on Chitral's *deck (1930s). The quantities of mail carried by P&O were enormous; the Christmas post for 1938 (the last in peacetime) ran to 12,000 bags.*

'Week by week, the many links in the great chain tautened and took the strain, from the village postman emptying a letter-box in a country lane to the P&O liner punctually keeping her rendezvous at Cap Janet, drawing the great mail trains to herself down the railroads of Europe like steel filings attracted to a magnet.'

CAPTAIN D. G. BAILLIE, 1953

'*MARSEILLES! The name conveys little to young Mail Officers of to-day… but to those of us who are a little older it conjures up memories of much hard work…. It had a special significance, too, as the starting point of the voyage; not only did the majority of our passengers – and the more important ones as a rule – join us there by the Overland Route across France, but it was in Marseilles that we loaded the Mails.*'

CAPTAIN D. G. BAILLIE, 1953

Rawalpindi *at Marseilles. Mail arriving by land would be sorted and counted by the Company's mail officer before being hoisted in slings and lowered into the holds.*

LONDON-MARSEILLES

'*This great train, which used to be considered one of the most luxurious in Europe, ran every week in connection with the outward and homeward mail ships.*'

CAPTAIN D. G. BAILLIE, 1953

Left: Brochure for the P&O Overland Express (cover design by Michael Horan).

P&O EXPRESS - LONDON MARSEILLES - 22 HR

THE 'OVERLAND ROUTE'

P&O found it relatively easy to fulfil the first Peninsular mail contract having already established agents and contacts in Spain and Portugal. What was to be altogether more challenging (and potentially lucrative) for the Company was the Admiralty's desire that a regular mail steam service be established beyond Egypt to India within two years of the 1840 Alexandria contract. This was an enormous undertaking, which required the construction of larger steam vessels capable of withstanding the monsoons of the Indian Ocean and a network of coal depots to fuel them; and there was the considerable problem of crossing the miles of desert which stood between Alexandria and Suez.

In 1840 Arthur Anderson made the first of a number of 'special missions' to Egypt returning to argue, with enthusiastic vigour, for the construction of a canal, for which he prepared a pamphlet for Parliament. A canal would of course be built, but not for another thirty years. In the meantime another entrepreneurial gentleman in Egypt had made the difficult desert crossing very much his own.

Lieutenant Thomas Waghorn had left the Navy in 1824, aged twenty-four, and had found work in India, having at one time commanded one of the Honourable East India Company's ships. He was a young man with ambition and a mission – to run the fastest mail courier service between England and India. By 1829, after much badgering of influential people, he received a permit to convey government dispatches across Egypt to India by the so-called 'overland route'.

Above: Lieut. Waghorn pioneered the overland route at a time when only a handful of adventurous travellers dared attempt the journey across the Egyptian desert. (Sir George Hayter) Opposite: For the first part of the route passengers travelled on the Mahmoudie Canal in small horse-drawn boats to Atfeh. (Henry Fitzcook)

'Once in the enjoyment of the Pasha's friendship I was enabled to establish mails to India and to keep the service in my own hands for four years. On one occasion I succeeded in getting letters from Bombay to England in 46 days by means of a fast French brig hired by me from Alexandria lying in ballast and ready to start at a moment's notice for Marseilles.'
Lieutenant Thomas Waghorn

William Makepeace Thackeray encountered Waghorn in 1844 and penned a wickedly sarcastic picture of the frenetic energy, the hustle and bustle, and the general conceit of the man:

'Lieutenant Waghorn is bouncing in and out of the courtyard full of business. He only left Bombay yesterday morning, was seen in the Red Sea on Tuesday, is engaged to dinner this afternoon in Regent's Park and (as it is about two minutes since I saw him in the courtyard) I make no doubt he is by this time at Alexandria or at Malta, say, perhaps at both.'
William Makepeace Thackeray, 1846

In the early days P&O had little choice but to follow Waghorn's route, which consisted of a complicated number of stages infinitely better suited to a parcel than a person. Leaving the P&O steamer at Alexandria, the first stage was to board small boats on the Mahmoudieh Canal which met the Nile at Atfeh. The boats were drawn by horses and controlled by a series of ropes that had to be lifted over the top of any passing sailing craft. From Atfeh small steamers made the sultry journey up the Nile to Cairo.

'There were two principal cabins, one for the ladies and the other for the gentlemen, there were sofas on which you could sit during the night to sleep or if you chose to keep on deck (which many did) there were mattresses to lay on, but the heavy dews are so unhealthy you catch colds, fevers and other sickness by doing it. It is, however, very delicious as the cabins are scarcely bearable for heat...'
Diary of Java-bound Engineer, September 1846

For the hundred miles of desert remaining, from Cairo to Suez, a train of camels carried the mail, whilst passengers climbed into horse-drawn carriages, the exact complement of passengers in each carriage having been drawn by lots when aboard ship. The carriages or 'vans' were open-sided with canvas roofs which meant taller passengers had to stoop.

'These vans contained six persons each and are built in a rough manner. They are like a rude omnibus on two large wheels and are drawn by four horses...the sittings in the vans are placed lengthways so that passengers sit face to face and two vans would always go together to assist each other in case of need. On crossing the desert we changed seven times, horses at station houses placed for the purpose about 10 or 12 miles apart. At No.2, No.4 and No.6 station houses you get refreshments.'
Diary of Java-bound Engineer, September 1846

Crossing the desert took three days, with twelve hours for rest and refreshment, and had all the highs and lows of an arduous adventure.

'At last we were off. Four huge vans full of passengers rattled out of the square, with a whoop and a shout, a waving of hats and kerchiefs, and many a hearty farewell, and safe journey from the bystanders...We dashed through the town in gallant style; the horses galloping and prancing, and our vans pitching and rolling like so many ships in a storm'.
Captain Albert Hervey, 1846

For some the arrival into Suez brought little relief:

'The wretchedness of Suez has often been described but never in terms too severe; the hotels belonging to the rival agents... are both uncomfortable. In Hill's [a competitor of Waghorn's] the accommodation...is of the worst kind... and the ultimate resort is the divan or a large cushioned seat of the dining room, and the cold night air from the desert freely blowing on the sleepers from the numerous panes of broken glass.'
Anonymous traveller, 1841

P&O was equally dissatisfied with Waghorn's and Hill's arrangements and deeply concerned by the popular misapprehension that the overland 'facilities' were those of the Company. Anderson began by establishing a good relationship with the Pasha, Egypt's ruler, without whom little could be done. Then he saw to it that the passage along the Mahmoudieh Canal was improved by the introduction of a steam tug (P&O's first twin screw vessel), which was built in England and shipped out to Egypt in pieces. New Nile steamers were built and a lock was constructed at Atfeh to ease the transfer from the canal to the river.

In time, Anderson persuaded the Pasha to surface some of the carriage route across the desert and saw to it that the rest houses (or staging posts) were both increased in

The desert crossing was broken up with rest houses where P&O provided food and drink. Central Station was the largest staging post en route. (Henry Fitzcook)

'Still the experience was one which impressed the imagination in no ordinary degree. A moonlight journey was most striking. The seemingly boundless expanse, the silence only broken by the voice of the driver and the muffled sound of horses' feet…then the sudden daybreak, the solitary Bedouin family mounted aloft on their desert ship…'

THOMAS SUTHERLAND, 1856

Encounters with nomadic Bedouin families enlivened the experience of crossing the desert. (Henry Fitzcook)

'The great bulk of our steamer passing through the narrow channel pushes a bow wave upon the flat margins of the Canal, which meets, in receding, the stern wash from the screw, the two together forming a formidable roller that surges back alongside the vessel and eats the banks away in a decidedly menacing manner. The sooner M. de Lesseps increases the width of his canal, the better...'

EDWIN ARNOLD, *PARRAMATTA*, 1899

number and bettered in facilities. Other improvements were already in hand:

'His Highness has granted the Company firmans for navigating both the Nile and the Canal by Steam – has established telegraphs [signal stations] across the desert; and is now taking measures to erect a Coal Depot at Alexandria, and a large Hotel at Suez, at the expense of the Egyptian government, the former for the Company's use, and the latter for the accommodation of passengers'
P&O Annual Report, 30th November 1842

Egypt was vital to P&O and good relations with its rulers even more so. In the 1850s the Company made generous loans to Pasha Ismail to fund the Alexandria to Cairo railway, which was completed in 1856. When a further extension of the railway was opened in 1859, it fell to the novelist Anthony Trollope, then a senior official of the Post Office, to negotiate with the Egyptian ruler for the mail to be carried on from Cairo to Suez.

EAST OF SUEZ

P&O's establishments at Suez had to be rather more extensive than those in the Mediterranean ports. Not only were the ships for India, and beyond, much larger, to carry more passengers and cargo over a longer route, but there was the problem of supplying them with coal, fresh water and provisions. There were no coal resources east of Suez so a store of at least 6,000 tons had to be maintained (and carried round the Cape or across the desert on camels).

As Thomas Sutherland noted in 1856, en route to his P&O posting in Hong Kong, water was also in scant supply:

'Nor is it, perhaps, the least vivid recollection that hardly more than a teacupful of water could be obtained at Suez for the purpose of ablution after this weary journey.'
Thomas Sutherland, 1856

The Company not only installed a water-condensing plant at Suez, but an ice-making machine and washing machines for the ships' linen. By necessity, Suez became a major port for victualling, with large food stores for supplies arriving from England, and outlying farms, including Goshen Farm close to Cairo, set up to supply fresh poultry, vegetables and fruit.

Despite initial misgivings, P&O steamers could be seen moving slowly through the canal by the mid-1870s. Assam *passes another vessel in the narrow waterway.*

CHAS. PEARS.

'The Suez Canal is one of
the wonders of the world,
and presents a picturesque
panorama of surpassing interest
as the ship slowly passes
through its tortuous length.
In the distance may be seen
the white and pink flamingoes,
together with innumerable
pelicans, while the long
processions of camels move
along the banks at intervals
on either side. As the average
width of the Canal is only 25
yards these objects, strange
and interesting to European
eyes, may be distinctly viewed.'

HARRY FURNISS, 1898

*The sight of the Company's steamers passing through the canal, dwarfing their surroundings as they grew in size, was impressive. (*Ranchi *by Charles Pears)*

With so much investment in infrastructure in Egypt it is not altogether surprising that P&O resented the opening of the Suez Canal when it came in 1869.

For the Indian and onward mail steamers, Aden became the main coaling port. Described as the 'key to the Red Sea', Aden represented a strategic coup for the British who had recently secured it. The American Commissioner to China, the Honourable Caleb Cushing, observed impartially in 1844:

'Aden is even more than Gibraltar a castle of nature's own construction. At Gibraltar, England has excavated herself a citadel in the heart of a limestone mountain. At Aden she has planted herself in an ancient crater and sits secure within the primeval fortress formed of the lofty sides of an extinct volcano.'
Hon Caleb Cushing, 1844

From slipways to sheep, P&O was well provided for at Aden with repair workshops, a water condensing plant, vast coal stores, a small steamer and a stock of at least twenty 'lighters' for coaling. To those who witnessed it first-hand, coaling was an extraordinary, labour-intensive sight:

'Our steamer took in about 200 tons of coal which laid ready for her in sacks stowed in iron lighters, it took 30 hours to take them over which is done by African Kolies. They sing 30 hours long such an unfavourable and doleful tune...that with the warmth, the coal dust and the song of the Kolies it's enough to make one go mad.'
Diary of Java-bound Engineer, *Precursor*, 1846

The P&O Agent and his staff occupied a large compound acquired by the Company in 1855. High above sea level the 'bungalow' at Steamer Point had commanding views of Aden harbour and a large masthead flying the P&O flag when a Company ship was in port.
Agency staff were responsible for keeping the mail on schedule and all aspects of ship, freight and passenger needs while they passed through Aden:

'The two guns from the fort have just gone off signifying that the mail boat has entered the fair-way...There is great excitement as the new Resident General is arriving on her, and there is to be an official reception on the quay...Already the band has started to play'.
W. F. Law Johnson, 23rd September 1919

More often than not the Agent was a recently retired senior P&O liner Captain, and *'in keeping with that august rank, a*

monocle was required uniform.' As masters of the Company's 'outposts' the Chief Agent was answerable to Head Office, regional rulers and at times the Empire.

'In 1931, Aden, although a British colony, was under the jurisdiction of the Government of India, but although the Viceroy held administrative sway, there is little doubt that the P&O Agent regarded his own status as second only to the Governor in residence.'
Sir Andrew Crichton, 1986

For the assistant clerk in an agency post, the work was hard, and anything but routine, but there were perks. Even the most junior employees were better paid than their counterparts in Head Office and able to afford a servant and membership of the 'club':

'The band plays down there on the terrace on Tuesday and Saturday evenings and on those occasions all the elite of Aden dine there.'
W. F. Law Johnson, 23rd September 1919

Having built up the necessary facilities at the western end of the Indian mail route, P&O turned its attention further east to Ceylon.

'Nothing can be more beautiful than the first sight of Ceylon, or more thoroughly impress him with the idea that he is in a tropical climate...I should think Galle was a very quiet place — it is by no means large and contains few Europeans...The Hotel is the best I have seen since we left Southampton. We dined at 7 o'clock. I think about 80 sat down together — some going home from Australia and India — others going outward to China, Bombay and Madras, some few were residents — in fact as motley a crew as you can well conceive.'
William Adamson, *Himalaya*, 1st March 1854

The location of Ceylon made it a natural port for transhipment of mail, cargo and passengers from P&O's various services to and from India, Egypt, China and Australia. The first Company ship to arrive at Point de Galle was *Hindostan* on her maiden positioning voyage from Southampton to India via the Cape. Among the passengers on the historic voyage was the young son of P&O's first agent at Galle who published an account of his journey some seventy years later:

'Galle was not then the great port it became afterwards and might then perhaps have been styled a 'fishing village' with some straw

Coal had to be shipped to wherever it was needed. In 1866 P&O estimated 170 ships were engaged annually in moving coal, not to mention the thousands of labourers.

Coaling a Steamer at Port Said.

'The approach of "The English Mail" was in those days signalled by the firing of cannon. This pleasant, time-honoured custom served to warn all local officials concerned with the mail ship's arrival, in particular the Harbour Master and the Post-master. It also brought home to those who had put off the writing of their letters that they had but one hour to complete this task.'

JACK HARLEY REMINISCING IN SEPTEMBER 1953

Arcadia *arriving in Aden in the 1950s. The arrival of turbo-electric and diesel engines removed the need for coaling, but Aden remained a port of call en route to Australia until 1970.*

'It would be difficult to imagine contrast more complete, as opposite sides of Creation, than Aden and Ceylon, the former like a vision of some ruined world, the latter the very ideal of Eden. Long before we sighted the beautiful isle the breath of these tropical forests met us out on the seas...'

GORDON-CUMMING, C.1860

The distinctive verdant scenery of Point de Galle painted in 1846. (Andrew Nicholl)

of truth, but certainly not as it often was after it became one of the chief ports of the East with its harbour crowded with steamers.'
Sir William Twynam, 1916

Hindostan appeared to dwarf the local boats in her wake:

"The arrival of so huge a leviathan as our steamer, amongst the small craft, caused them to jump about as if for very joy at her coming."
Captain Albert Hervey, 1846

P&O's Agent, Thomas Twynam, came to Ceylon as a young man and had previously been Superintendent at the Port of Trincomalee where he met and married his wife Mary Cecilia. The role of Agent's wife in far flung outposts was often a familial one, providing a home for Agency clerks and Company officers passing through. Such was the 'motherly kindness' and hospitality shown by Mary Twynam to P&O officers that they erected a monument in her honour, at the Dutch church in Galle, following her death in 1853.

Twynam was followed by Captain Francis Bayley, who served loyally as P&O's Agent for some forty years. During this time the Company moved its base from Galle to Colombo, some seventy miles north, in 1882. The new artificial harbour at Colombo had less of the charm of Galle, but P&O had a commanding white stone office in the centre of the town. The Agency continued until the 1930s when it had the distinction of being the last of the P&O Agencies to be taken over by first Earl of Inchcape 'for inclusion in his own chain'. His own chain was Mackinnons, which he now controlled, and which had opened an office in Colombo in 1917.

India had long been in P&O's sights, and the arrival of *Hindostan* in Calcutta, in the closing days of 1842, was a major achievement for the Company. Soon P&O were running a regular mail service using *Hindostan*, *Bentinck* and *Precursor*.

The Company quickly established a solid base in Calcutta where the English inhabitants numbered over 3,000 and '*divided for the most part into merchants, trades-people, civil and military staff, officers, lawyers and persons employed by the shipping trade, and others*'. At the time of the Indian Mutiny, the Company's employees raised their own squadron calling themselves the 'Bengal Yeomanry', albeit most of them had never been on a horse.

Although Calcutta was the seat of Government, Bombay was the merchant's capital of India and it was here that P&O

In 1861 the Company's Agent, Captain Bayley built himself a house, idyllically located at Galle, later selling it to P&O, which retained it until 1889. (Artist unknown)

'In spite of the hot climate, Ceylon is one of the most charming spots on the face of the earth, and teems with picturesqueness and interest. No traveller, armed with a pith helmet, a good white umbrella lined with green or blue, light clothes, and a heavy purse, should on any account miss seeing it.'

HARRY FURNISS, 1898

most wanted to establish its principal base. But Bombay 'belonged' to the Honourable East India Company and having enjoyed a monopoly on all things east of Suez since its foundation in the seventeenth century, it was doggedly defending it. P&O persisted, establishing a presence in Bombay in 1847, and sending steamers on speculative runs between Bombay and Galle. In the end it was the Admiralty who lost patience with the irregular services of the Honourable Company and by 1854 the Bombay mails had passed to P&O, enabling it to run a weekly mail service alternating between Calcutta and Bombay.

Bombay was more strategically positioned than Calcutta for P&O to pursue new services to China, including the trade in opium and silk. P&O made Bombay its main repairing facility in the East, establishing the Magazon Dock on reclaimed land, workshops, warehouses, offices and an ice-making plant (capable of producing three tons of ice a day); and employing a very sizeable local workforce.

The city's importance was evidenced by the sheer amount of mail P&O handled, which by the 1880s was estimated at 73,000 items a year. Bombay was also a major port for freight and passengers many of whom resided in Bombay and saw P&O as a tangible link to home:

'The Royal Bombay Yacht Club…would be crowded on Friday evenings with members, and more particularly their wives, anxious to inspect the latest cold weather visitors and the newest fashions from Home, just landed that morning, from the weekly P&O steamer!'
Captain D. G. Baillie, 1953

With a presence in Bombay and Calcutta P&O was able to promote 'tours' through India in the 'off season' (using the extensive railway network) to passengers arriving and departing by P&O steamer. In peak season, when time was at a premium, the Company ran a seasonal corridor train known as the 'P&O Limited Boat Express' from Bombay to Delhi. The train was fitted with 'baths, electric light and fans' and accommodated first-class passengers (and their servants) only. All this could be arranged, tickets bought and 'coupes' reserved, from London. The very operation of P&O in India depended on the mails as much as any other business.

'…Britishers should also remember the P&O is one of Bombay's greatest assets, great ships leaving and arriving every week loaded with freight and passengers. Hats off to the great P&O!'
American passenger, 1937

The Ceylon motor map was the first of its kind to be produced by the Company in 1908.

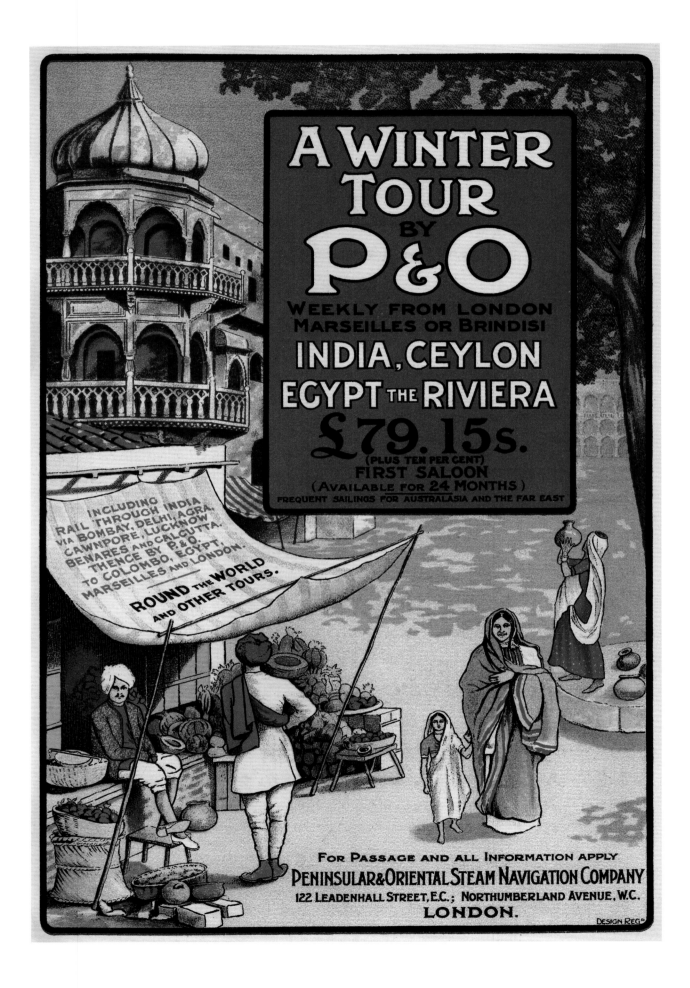

THE FAR EAST & AUSTRALIA

Singapore was first visited by a P&O ship, *Lady Mary Wood*, on the 4th August 1845. Stamford Raffles had hoisted the flag of the East India Company on the island in 1819 and its natural harbour and position, lying between India and China, made it a key agency for P&O.

By 1852 the Company's Ceylon to Singapore service was well underway. The first P&O Agent, Captain T. Marshall, soon found that the harbour facilities were becoming inadequate. He bought a site and set about draining it and clearing it of jungle before building a coal shed, offices and the first wharf (Keppel). P&O became an important part of the community and had an impressive four-storey office, in an arcaded Venetian style, in the heart of Singapore.

As well as the mail, the Company's ships frequently carried special Admiralty dispatches often arriving too late for P&O's precise hour of departure. It was not uncommon in the early days for Admirals to take drastic measures, insisting that the mail steamers wait upon their readiness:

'The Master of the P&O steamer in Singapore in 1867, having made some demur as to waiting a short time to take Admiral Keppel's dispatches on board, was actually prevented from going to sea, if he had intended to do so, by a manned-and-armed cutter being laid alongside the vessel at the New Harbour Wharf; the letters, however, were on board before the advertised hour for sailing.'
T. A. Melville, 1921

Nearly a century after P&O first arrived in the colony the Company was still playing an important role. As the Japanese were invading Singapore in the Second World War, the government called upon P&O to co-ordinate the evacuation of those leaving by sea. Fearing that the P&O offices and waiting crowds would be the target of bomb attacks, the Company's passage clerks, and their local colleagues, were set up in a safe house in Cluny where they:

'sat at tables, handing out embarkation slips as fast as they could write. They waived questions of payment and there were no favours. Those P&O men did a twenty-four hour job… They were a credit to their Company.'
Kenneth Attiwill, 1959

Those 'P&O men' – Frank Hammond, Charles Jenkins and Philip Barnes – were later taken prisoner by the Japanese and the Company's offices destroyed.

Opposite: Colourful brochure from 1907, one of many designed to lure the British public away from the cold of winter. Above: The P&O office in Calcutta.

> *'It used to be said, and I think it is so, that memories of the first posting in the East are indelible.'*
>
> SIR ANDREW CRICHTON, 1986

'The P&O dockyards here are acknowledged to be the best kept and neatest place of any kind in the East, and I may say I think in the world. There is no dry dock, but works, carpenters, blacksmiths etc, etc, shops, and coal sheds, all as clean and neat as a new pin....'

F. R. KENDALL, 27TH SEPTEMBER, 1859

In Singapore P&O helped create the port infrastructure by building a wharf and jetties at New harbour, which were all in place by the 1860s.

'Sutherland…a little king in Hong Kong and all over China both amongst the English and the Chinamen. Even the biggest Chinaman would lose face…if he were not on good footings with the P&O – which out here means 'S'.'

F. R. KENDALL, DECEMBER 1863

When P&O's *Lady Mary Wood* arrived in Hong Kong in 1845 the colony had only recently been ceded to Britain three years earlier in 1842. For a short time Hong Kong marked the extent of the Company's reach and completed a chain of strategic ports, linking the Red Sea to China. In Victoria the Company erected one of its grandest offices yet, with a distinctive cast-iron verandah, giving rise to the Chinese name for P&O – 'tit hong' – strong, iron house.

It was some ten years after P&O's arrival in the colony that the young Thomas Sutherland was sent out to the Company's office. Hong Kong was much less developed than many of the other ports en route, and still considered unhealthy and dangerous, but as a free port it provided important opportunities for trade with China and Japan. The presence of Sutherland did much to elevate the importance of the Hong Kong office, and junior employees began to compete to go there, just to work under the 'little king':

'The P&O as a rule take a higher standing here than they do elsewhere in the East. This is to a great extent Sutherland's doing, and as he has always had some good men with him since he has been in charge of the agency, he has been able to maintain a good standard.'
F. R. Kendall, 12th December 1863

Hong Kong was to be one of P&O's most continuous bases. Long after the 'iron house' ceased to exist, the Company built an impressive tower block on the waterfront housing both P&O and Mackinnons (established in Hong Kong since 1919).

In 1992 the Company's Chairman spoke of the close affinity P&O shared with Hong Kong:

'… in Hong Kong people look forward as do we in P&O. Optimism and confidence is the very air that you breathe and it is the air that we breathe. It was in this spirit that last year P&O received a listing on the Hong Kong Stock Exchange. It is why, earlier this year, P&O Asia Ltd., was established with its headquarters in Hong Kong. And today P&O Containers is the largest container shipper to and from Hong Kong.'
Lord Sterling, 1992

In 1850 P&O opened a branch service from Hong Kong to Shanghai and established a foothold in mainland China. It was part of a long held strategy and it neatly brought steam and P&O into the lucrative opium trade. Like tea, opium was shipped in fast sailing ships, or clippers, and their owners and agents were extremely concerned by growing

The Chinese name for P&O – 'iron house' – derived from the distinctive cast-iron balcony on the Company's office, built in Hong Kong between 1844 and 1852. (Artist unknown)

'A voyage to China is a very different thing now to what it was seventy or even twenty years ago. The modern ambassador to the court of the "Son of Heaven" packs his portmanteau and locks his despatch-box some afternoon in Belgravia. He takes a comfortable dinner, says good-by to his family, drives to London Bridge station, and in forty-eight hours he is smoking a cigar on the paddle-box of a Peninsular and Oriental Company's steamer, out of sight of land in the Mediterranean.'

BLACKWOOD'S EDINBURGH MAGAZINE, JANUARY, 1861

Named after Sir Henry Pottinger, the Governor General of Hong Kong in the early 1840's, Pottinger *operated between Bombay and Hong Kong. (J. F. Stace)*

An advertisement from 1932 (D. Wagstaff) and an elaborate brochure which was produced for the post-war resumption of passenger liner calls at Japan in 1954. (Kay Stewart)

competition particularly from faster steamers. P&O carried opium with considerable success, and the Company could lay claim to carrying the first tea ever shipped to England by steamer in 1859.

It was Sutherland who first investigated the possibility of extending P&O's interests into the unknown realms of Japan: *'the first time I landed in that country there were not more than three or four Englishmen there'*. Sutherland had arrived not on a P&O ship but 'a little opium schooner', belonging to Dent & Co, and running between Shanghai and Nagasaki. He returned to Hong Kong enthused and on his recommendation (which met with approval in London), the P&O steamer *Azof* began an experimental service on the Shanghai to Nagasaki route in 1859.

Yokohama, which was to be home to the Company's office in Japan, was first visited in 1860. At the time it was little more than a village, recently reclaimed from the sea, but it was one of the few Japanese ports where foreign ships were allowed to call and where foreigners were allowed to reside. The P&O office, a large bungalow in the Naka-Ku area, was opened in 1866. A year later the Company won the first mail contract for a fortnightly service between Yokohama and Shanghai, calling at Nagasaki. Cargo dominated the growth in services to Japan where P&O had a presence for over a century.

The Company's long association with Australia started when it won the mail contract in 1852:

'The success of the Indian Mail Service soon found an echo in Australia and an anxious desire was expressed to obtain for the Colonies the benefit of steam communication with the mother country as quickly as possible.'
Thomas Sutherland, 1888

In the same year *Chusan* sailed round the Cape of Good Hope to Sydney, arriving on 31st August 1852 to a rapturous welcome.

The early P&O service to Australia ran every other month, but when the Company's ships were needed to carry troops for the Crimean War, P&O was granted permission to abandon the service in favour of its more established routes. When the mail contract was being re-negotiated it went, for a short time, to a competitor, before returning to P&O in 1859. From then on the Company operated a regular mail service to Australia (which it shared with the Orient Line from 1883) right up to the Second World War. In time Australia was to become an important market for the P&O's freight trade and the home of its port developments.

'*...the P&O company's relations with Japan were to be marked by the resumption, for the first time since the end of the war, of the mail and passenger service. For this purpose, the latest and finest P&O vessel, the* Chusan *was to extend the voyage to Yokohama and Kobe. It was hoped that from this step there would accrue prestige and commercial benefit for British interests nationally, and for P&O particularly.'*

SIR ANDREW CRICHTON, 1986

Overleaf: P&O's Yokohama office at 14 Yamashita-Cho opened in 1866. In Japan P&O cultivated a market for mail, cargo and even ships that it wished to sell. (Kunitsuru)

In the early years of the twentieth century P&O became involved in emigration services to Australia for the first time. The P&O Branch Line (formerly Lund's Blue Anchor Line) ran the Company's emigrant and third-class service to Australia via the longer Cape route from 1910 up to 1930s. After the Second World War when the Australian government was energetically seeking to increase its working population, P&O provided berths for the burgeoning 'Ten Pound Poms' arriving in Australia on the assisted passage scheme running between 1945 and 1973. For thousands of 'poms', the P&O passage out was the last link between home and a new life down under.

By the end of the nineteenth century the Company had over seventy bases overseas, and a P&O guide book could justly claim:

'*Fifty years ago* [in 1841] *the whole trade of Great Britain with the East did not amount probably to more than £20,000,000. To-day* [1891], *it is at least equal to £160,000,000. What share the Company may have contributed towards the growth of this vast commerce, cannot, of course, be defined, but when it is remembered that for upwards of thirty-three years the Company was almost the exclusive courier by steam to India, China and Australia, and that during that period the correspondence, the exchanges, the transport of bullion and of more precious merchandise (to say nothing of the conveyance of passengers) depended entirely upon its organization and working, it may be claimed that its influence in fostering this trade has been equal if not greater than that of any other single agency...*'
P&O Guide book, 1891

With the 1914 merger with BI and the various other shipping lines acquired by Inchcape, P&O became even more entrenched in colonial trade with services extending to New Zealand and the Pacific, up the Gulf and down the East African Coast. In spite of radically having to alter course with 'the end of the Empire', by the new millennium P&O still maintained a worldwide presence, operating on every continent including Antarctica.

Mongolia *ran on the fortnightly service to Australia and was a regular sight in Sydney at No.4 Berth Circular Quay. (Photograph dated 1933)*

'I am going abroad to seek ships for immigrants. If we have no ships, we shall get no Immigrants, and without immigration, the future of the Australia we know will be both uneasy and brief. As a nation we shall not survive.'

ARTHUR CALWELL, 1945

Opposite: Departing on Stratheden *c.1950s. Above: Detail from a P&O poster advertising special 'boomerang' return fares to Australia c.1956. (Johnston)*

'The whole scheme of decoration must be sufficiently positive to give a definite personality to the ship equal to the individuality of its external form. The passenger should end his journey with positive pleasurable memories of the special world in which he has lived for days or weeks...' Misha Black, 1961

In 1837 the Company advertised its fleet of ships: *'...in their [the ships'] construction and machinery, every tried improvement has been adopted, without regard to expense. In the planning and layout of the accommodation, the comfort and convenience of passengers have to be studiously kept in view. The Saloons are very spacious and airy, and the Sleeping Cabins have been arranged so as to suit families or parties of friends from two up to eight in number... Each cabin is fitted with all the requisite conveniences for washing, dressing etc. and from each cabin a bell communicates with the Stewards and Servant's rooms. The Ladies' Cabins are tastefully fitted up and contain every necessary for the toilet.'*
Peninsular Steam Navigation Company, 2nd January 1837

But, as with most advertising, the reality was rather different. P&O's earliest ships were hard-working vessels, running to very tight schedules to carry the mail on time. The first steam engines were not particularly efficient, requiring vast amounts of coal to produce relatively little power. Of necessity, much of the space in the early Company steamers was taken up by the engine, the boiler, the paddles and the coal bunkers:

'We left [Mauritius] with every corner of the ship full of coal, and about 240 tons on deck, a not very agreeable thing, but still a necessary nuisance from the length of the voyage.'
F. R. Kendall, *Benares*, 21st April 1859

And then there was another fuel – the 'victualling' for passengers and crew. With no means of refrigeration and relatively few ports of call, certainly beyond Suez, meat had to be carried live and 'killed for the table as required'. The deck of the ships, crowded with cows, sheep, and poultry, resembled farmyards at sea. All this meant there was limited space for passengers. A main saloon catered for principal shipboard activities: eating and drinking, reading, writing and game playing. Typically the saloon was furnished with one or more long tables, shelves for crockery, a bookcase for the makeshift library, a fireplace or stove and sometimes a settee. What ventilation existed was provided by skylights, and lighting by candle. As a passenger on P&O's first ship on the Alexandria run noted in 1841, there was room for improvement: *'...the interior of the vessel is in my opinion ill-contrived. There is no proper partition between the large saloon and the main deck, so that the smell of hot oil, tallow, and the disagreeables from the cooking apparatus...the nausea also from the places where the stock is kept, came into the saloon. There is no cabin companion except a scuttle in the after part, so that passengers have to pass from the main deck into the cabin through all sorts of dirt and nuisance; indeed, the main deck was disgracefully dirty, a perfect pandemonium.'*
Captain Sir William Symonds RN, *Oriental*, 1841

An 'operatic company' bound for Egypt share Sumatra's *limited deck space with live animals which were a feature of P&O's early ships.* Illustrated London News, *November 1875.*

Below deck, space was even more limited and shared cabins were the norm:

'I now began to look after my berth and found (what I thought the day before a comfortable place) metamorphised into a miserable place. Six passengers stowed into a cabin fit only for two. Temporary berths were erected which made it so small. When in bed I could scarcely turn without interrupting another passenger, and if I moved my feet I kicked another in the head, so close we were crowded together. For the six of us there was only one washstand, one basin etc. and besides experiencing the inconvenience of waiting for each other, had actually not place sufficient to shave.'
Diary of Java-bound Engineer, *Oriental*, 20th August 1846

With the introduction of *Hindostan* and *Bentinck*, to operate the Calcutta run from Suez, there was a concerted effort to improve the disposition of the cabins, placing them in the centre of the ship to minimize the experience of pitching and rolling, and to increase the comfort and proportions of the saloon:

'The cuddy is a magnificent room, running as far aft as the stern posts, and as far forward as cabins and the situation of the engineroom would permit… The appearance of the whole was superb, when lighted of an evening, which it was with argaund lamps suspended from the ceiling; large mirrors at each end and book-cases, neatly fitted up, containing useful and entertaining works. The furniture is entirely mahogany, and the fastenings &c, of bronze.'
Captain Albert Hervey, *Hindostan*, 1846

For some such attentions to decorative details were misplaced:

'Perhaps too much money has been lavished on mere embellishments. Pictures and finely carved woodwork are on the whole of that part of the ship which is fitted up for passengers, most of whom would be glad to go in vessels with less costly decorations at a lower charge.'
Lady traveller, *Hindostan*, 1844

Unsurprisingly any enhancements to washing facilities, which at their most basic consisted of a basin (with water delivered daily by the stewards) were universally appreciated:

'There are baths on board, both shower and plunging; most delightful of a morning, after melting in our cabins, to be able to enjoy the one or the other.'
Captain Albert Hervey, *Hindostan*, 1846

P&O produced a colourful Fleet Book illustrating the interiors of its mail (and passenger) and 'intermediate' steamers. Clockwise from top left: A typical Dining Saloon of the 'N' class, Music Saloon of the 'Persia' class, Dining Room and Smoking Room of the 'D' class.

Above: In 1884 Valetta *became the first vessel to have electric lights fitted in the first-class saloons. (Frank Stewart Murray)*

This was a vast improvement for the regular traveller to India, in the 1840s, comparing the Company's steamers with the alternative of sailing ships 'crawling round the Cape, for a period of three or four months', and in which:

'*…if you do wish to have a bathe, you are obliged to stand at the break of the poop or gangway, to be soused with all the sailors with water, taken out of a dirty, greasy tub.'*
Captain Albert Hervey, *Hindostan*, 1846

The introduction of new ships with screw propellers into the P&O fleet increased the amount of deck and internal space available for passenger accommodation particularly in the centre of the ship (previously occupied by paddle boxes). The result was increasingly larger and more commodious saloons, as a passenger on *Himalaya* observed:

'*I inspected the saloon which is a very handsome room, fitted up with Maple, relieved by a gilt border with a panel of glass at intervals. The seats are covered with Crimson Velvet with a gilt heading. At the head of the saloon is a piano, and at the foot, between the two entrance doors, are a sideboard and a magnificent pier glass. Around the saloon are a number of elegantly fitted cabins, but from their situation they are not so comfortable as the "for'ard ones", the roll of the ship, and the noise of the screw being very unpleasant to their occupants.'*
William Adamson, *Himalaya*, 20th January 1854

With the opening of the Suez Canal in 1869 not only did P&O have to restore its immediate and significant losses in revenue, but also its reputation and its fleet. The Company required totally new ships, capable of traversing the entire passage from London to India and beyond to Australia and the Far East. The new vessels had to be altogether more sophisticated, both in terms of technical advances and interior design and to combine: '*large cargo capacity with that superior class of accommodation for passengers which has ever been afforded by the Company's steamers'.*

P&O's *Kaisar-i-Hind* ('Empress of India') was the largest and fastest addition to the fleet in 1878 and introduced a new level of comfort worthy of the post-Suez era of competition. The ship had a sizeable saloon lit with swinging oil lamps, a generous smoking room furnished with settees, considerably more communal bathrooms and, of key importance, an element of electricity, at least for cabin bells and refrigeration. The first-class saloon of *Valetta* was lit by electric light in 1884, the first P&O ship to be so equipped.

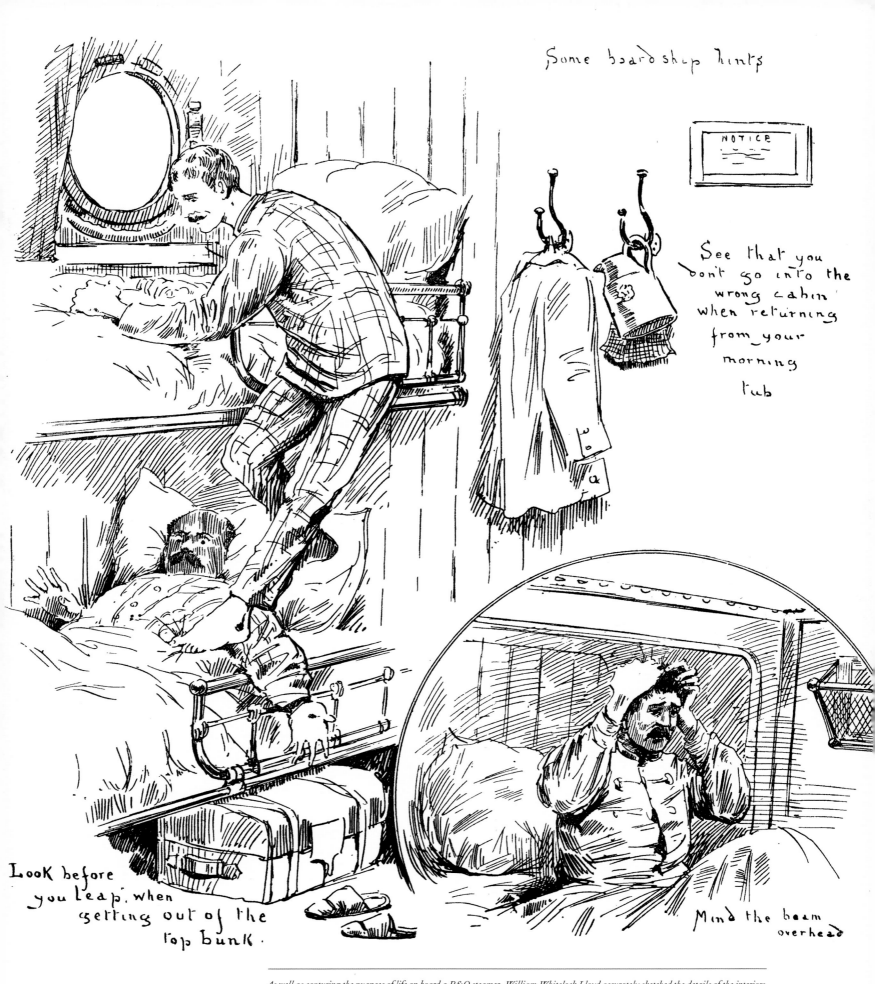

As well as capturing the nuances of life on board a P&O steamer, William Whitelock Lloyd accurately sketched the details of the interiors – the tiled smoking room (left) and the compact shared cabins (above) – of the 'Jubilee' liners and Mirzapore. (P&O Pencillings)

The last quarter of the nineteenth century saw not only the introduction of electricity, but a general expansion of public areas for diverse functions. In addition to the saloon for meals, there was a music room, a smoking room, a library, a surgery, a drying room and a barber's shop (which often doubled up as a shop for general provisions and gifts). There were even special photographic studios for the burgeoning interest of passengers in taking 'views'.

Such refinements were all aboard P&O's 'Jubilee' ships – *Britannia*, *Victoria*, *Oceana* and *Arcadia* – launched to coincide with Queen Victoria's, and the Company's, Jubilee in 1887. A reporter described the *Arcadia's* lofty interiors:

'Entering a door on the promenade (hurricane) deck we find ourselves at the head of the grand stairway leading down to the spar deck. Before descending we enter the music or drawing room – a room decorated in white and gold, charmingly carpeted and cushioned…at one end we looked down through a well into the saloon below. This large well… is adorned… by a beautiful stain-glass dome…. Descending by a double staircase we reach the spar

deck…this staircase and all the woodwork of the saloon are of oak while the ceiling is white and gold…. This saloon with its two main tables down the centre and smaller tables on the side seats 138; the chairs swing round in the usual way and have reversible seats, cane or velvet. Punkahs are fitted over the table in hot weather.'
Journalist, *Arcadia*, c.1890

'Punkahs' were sheets of jute, or similar material, sometimes covered with white linen, hanging from the ceiling with connected ropes that were pulled and operated by punkah-wallahs to create a cooling draught. With the introduction of electricity, the pulling mechanism was automated and, eventually, they were replaced by electric fans.

Of the *Britannia's* cabins, the *Scarborough Gazette* reported:

'The sleeping berths on the Britannia *are remarkable for their airiness and comfort, both in the first and second classes. They are arranged in two rows, the outer ones, next the skin of the vessel, being, of course, the better lighted, as a large porthole opens into each one. The fittings are simple but elegant,*

Above: A typical two-berth cabin or stateroom with washstand on Britannia. *The basic design of cabins remained largely unchanged for a further quarter of a century but as the size of ships grew, more berths were located above the waterline.*

Opposite: A sweeping double staircase, decorated with a pair of bronze sculptures by Frank Lynn-Jenkins, separated the First Class Music Room from the Dining Saloon on board Maloja. *(c. 1911)*

consisting of spring mattresses, patent folding washstands and a chest of drawers. The latter introduction is a welcome novelty, and very convenient, as each passenger is provided with a drawer, numbered to correspond with the berth'.
Scarborough Gazette, *Britannia*, 9th February 1888

The 'patent folding washstand' was described in detail by a P&O purser in 1907:

'The main item was a weird arrangement like a coffin standing on end; on the top it had a bracket to hold a glass for drinking water and two tumblers; a hole to pour water into a tank which was faced by a looking glass, and underneath this a basin could be let down, exposing a tap.'
Ashley Randall

Until the end of the century, it was usual for the commissioning ship-owner and the yard to agree the general scheme for decoration of a new ship. The actual fitting out would then be carried out by local craftsmen, under the direction of the shipyard, or in time carried out by specialist furniture and furnishing firms such as Waring & Gillows.

It was not until the 1890s that P&O made regular use of a 'professional' designer – Thomas Edward Collcutt. Collcutt was not only an architect but a furniture designer (along Arts and Crafts lines) and was engaged in designing Sir Thomas Sutherland's country home in the late 1880s. It was this connection to the then Chairman which in all probability earned Collcutt his first P&O commission to design the Company's pavilion for the Royal Naval Exhibition in London in 1891. The pavilion had an exotic 'chinoise' appearance and included a fully-fitted smoking saloon destined for P&O's latest steamer *Australia*.

Collcutt transferred his design skills from shore to ship working on the interiors of no fewer than twelve P&O ships launched between 1896 and 1913, including the five 'Persia' class vessels – *India, China, Egypt, Arabia* and *Persia*. Collcutt continued to use the services of the celebrated ceramicist William De Morgan, first employed on a P&O ship in 1882. Tiles made a perfect addition to the smoking rooms and companionways, where they were cool in warm weather and easily cleaned. Being inspired by Middle Eastern colours and scenes, particularly Iznik, they fitted the general Persian theme of decoration that pervaded many P&O ships of the time. De Morgan recounted that he viewed the P&O commissions with mixed feelings, having found the P&O Board 'a highly meddlesome, pragmatic body'.

Maloja's impressive barrel-vaulted ceiling, high above the galleried music room and the dining room below, was richly decorated with murals by Professor Gerald Moira. (c. 1911)

'...tales of a dining room ceiling of heavy decorative tiles (from De Morgan, I have always hoped) which started, in rough weather, dropping one by one like ripe pears, so that for the rest of the voyage meals had to be eaten crouched beneath the dubious protection of a stretched velarium of netting into which from time to time yet another tile would bounce.'

SIR COLIN ANDERSON, JUNE 1967

For the first-class saloons of the earlier 'Persia' class ships (above), William De Morgan produced colourful and elaborate tiled panels. Between 1882 and 1900 De Morgan worked on twelve P&O liners including the First Class Smoking Room on Arabia *(right).*

One wonders whether Collcutt encountered similar frustrations or whether, as one P&O employee recalled, it was the designer who had the upper hand: '*I remember how difficult he was to handle if it was necessary to go contrary to his ideas.*' Collcutt went on to design for many of the 'M' class ships including *Moldavia, Mongolia, Marmora, Macedonia, Morea* and, later, *Medina*, where he was responsible for the royal suite of apartments. Like the 'Jubilee' ships, the 'M' class ships were mostly built either in the Scottish yard of Sutherland's great friend Sir James Caird (in his Greenock constituency) or at the Harland and Wolff yard in Belfast. Other designers involved included the sculptor Frank Lynn-Jenkins and the muralist Professor Gerald Moira. Lynn-Jenkins' bronzes filled the niches of the wood panelled walls, whilst Moira's vast murals decorated the lunettes of the barrel-vaulted glazed ceilings of the first-class saloons.

The 'M' class ships were a product of their time. They carried more passengers at faster speeds than the 'Persia' class and were able for the first time to make use of Marconi's invention of wireless telegraphy, albeit sometimes for less than essential purposes. In 1910 the passengers of *Mantua* travelling east from Fremantle to Adelaide played chess against those of *Morea* travelling west. The game was conducted by wireless telegraphy and lasted six hours, *Mantua* taking the honours in twenty-one moves.

Between ships, Collcutt was busy ashore designing hotels including one in Colombo and extending the P&O Head Office in Leadenhall Street. Collcutt had made his maritime mark with the Company, and with new offices for Lloyd's Register of Shipping, but he is best remembered in London as the architect of the Imperial Institute (of which only the tower remains today) and the Wigmore Hall and Palace Theatre (originally the English Opera House), which are both still intact.

With the introduction of cruising in 1904, there was one Company ship adapted entirely to meet the specific needs of passengers travelling purely for pleasure. *Vectis* had begun life as the P&O mail steamer *Rome*, which was first lengthened and later refitted and renamed as the Company's first 'touring yacht'. Edward Rawdin, who was to take a number of cruises in *Vectis*, was fulsome in his praises of her facilities:

'*The company has, at great expense, turned her into one of the most comfortable yachts afloat; there are beautiful drawing and lounge rooms, the finest smoking room we have ever seen, the dining saloon is splendidly situated…* [of their cabin neighbour,

Narkunda's *First Class Music Room in 1920. The First Class Dining Room was equally impressive and decorated with Professor Gerald Moira's most elaborate murals for P&O.*

Typical First Class Music Room (top), Companion (middle) and Dining Saloon (bottom) found in the 'M' class steamers. (Illustrated in 1907)

Morea, launched in 1908 at Cairds in Greenock, was the sixth of the ten liners which made up the 'M' class. (Bernard Finegan Gribble)

the barber] *his shop is the largest we have ever seen on any ship… The promenade deck is very spacious, eight times round it a mile.'*
Edward Rawdin, *Vectis*, c.1910

P&O passengers were growing increasingly discerning in their tastes and expectations of onboard facilities and comforts. The first Earl of Inchcape travelled regularly on the Company's ships, often accompanied by his wife or one of his daughters, and was aware of the need to keep step with the demands of passengers. Embarking on a new class of ships, he found a design solution close to home:

'I feel some diffidence on assenting to my daughter being given this appointment but I conscientiously believe it will be a good thing for the P&O Company – we are building ships, which unless they come to grief will be on the service for the next twenty years, and we have to look ahead. None of our older vessels have the conveniences which people nowadays require. They have no wardrobe, passengers have to keep their clothes in trunks underneath their bunks… the lights are not arranged so as to be convenient, the looking glasses are badly placed, the arrangements for the wash hand basins are inefficient and inconvenient (and) the public rooms… arranged and furnished without any regard to taste.'
Lord Inchcape, 29th April 1925

The daughter in question was the Honourable Elsie Mackay. She was clearly a girl of some talent and certainly seems to have epitomised 1920s glamour. She had appeared in some eight films between 1920 and 1921 under the name Poppy Wyndham, having eloped and married a fellow actor. She was daring and contrary as she galloped her horses, drove her Rolls Royce rather fast and took to the skies in her Avro biplane, all one presumes with some panache and, as the daughter of a prominent Earl in society, some notoriety.

But what of design? One perhaps needs to look to hidden agendas to understand Inchcape's confidence in his daughter's as yet untested design potential. Through her early escapades Elsie had been cut off by the family, but by 1925 there seems to have been both a rapprochement and a divorce. A new focus would keep Elsie close at hand and provide an outlet for her abundant and restless energy. As a sop to P&O, it was agreed that Elsie's salary would be taken out of Inchcape's emoluments.

Initially Elsie, and her mother, were 'let loose' on P&O's *Razmak*, launched in 1924 by Lady Inchcape, for the Aden to Bombay shuttle service. But it was with *Viceroy of India*

Overleaf: Among over 300 Viceroy *items in the collection is a special ship model made by P&O's Tommy Dring who travelled between ships playing in the ship's band and making models for the Company.*

P&O
CRUISES
The New Turbo-Electric S.S.
"VICEROY OF INDIA"
19,500 tons

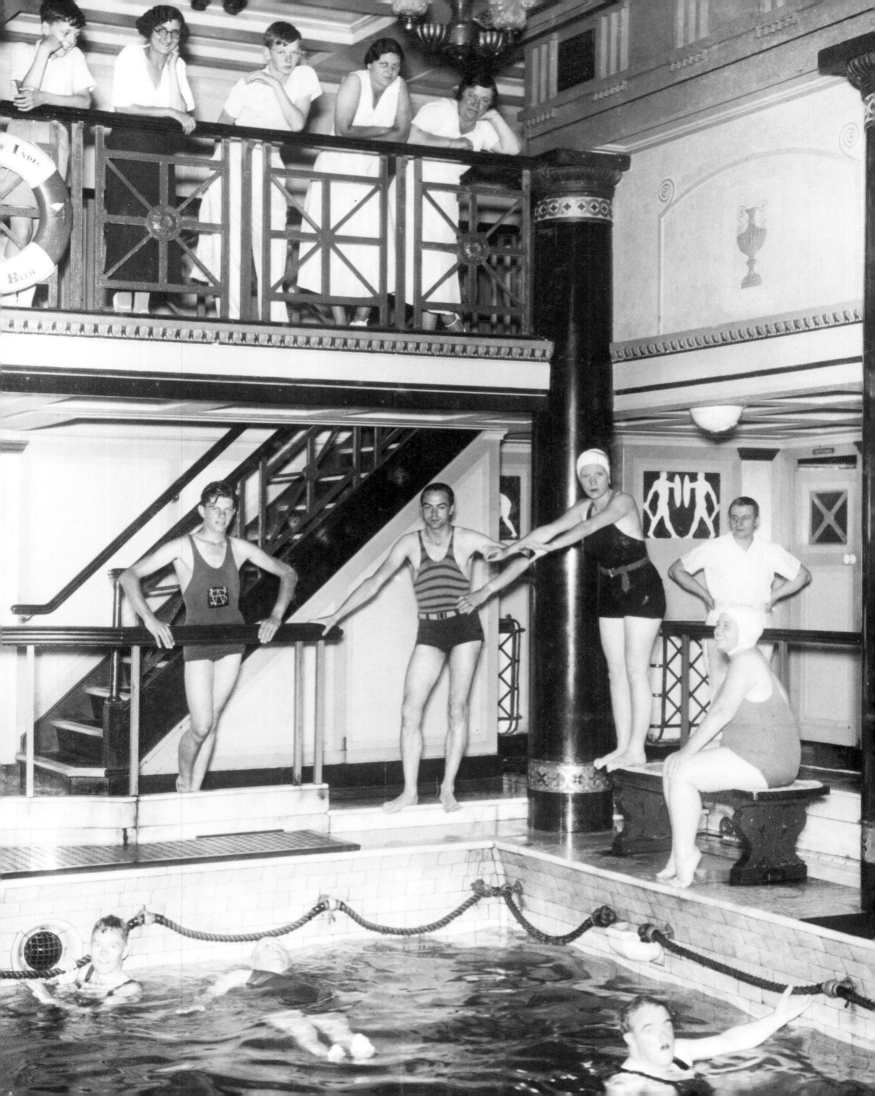

that Elsie was to make her mark and leave her legacy. Whilst 'Viceroy' was still on the stocks Elsie, unbeknown to all, and particularly her father, was busy planning her attempt to be the first woman to fly the Atlantic. With her parents conveniently in Egypt, Elsie and her co-pilot took to the skies in March 1928 and were never seen again. For Inchcape the launch of *Viceroy of India* six months later must have evoked mixed feelings.

Inchcape's intent, at a time of faltering fortunes for the Company, was that *Viceroy of India* should be as technically advanced as practicable, and as luxurious as budget would allow. He succeeded on both counts. Hailed as the first European-owned, turbo-electric-driven liner, *Viceroy of India* generously accommodated 415 first class passengers in the luxury of single-berthed cabins or 'cabines-de-luxe' with private bathrooms. Outside, there was a gargantuan sports deck and, inside, a swimming pool – the first of its kind on a P&O liner.

Despite Elsie's own pioneering spirit, in terms of design she stuck firmly to the past and the 'historic'. The reading and writing room was Adamesque, the music room Neoclassical, the swimming pool Pompeian, the Verandah café Moorish and then there was the smoking room for which Elsie turned to the Jacobeans and James I's State Room of the Old Palace at Bromley-by-Bow from 1606, preserved in the Victoria and Albert Museum. The resulting room was festooned with oak panels and overmantels, caryatids, coats of arms, crossed swords, leaded windows and even a museum of Bonnie Prince Charlie's relics. The utter exuberance and over-elaboration of the ship's interiors was a reflection of Elsie's extravagant personality. *Viceroy of India* bore not even a hint of contemporary design movements, particularly nothing of the pared-down puritan 'fitness for purpose' of the Bauhaus design school.

Opposite: The indoor swimming pool on Viceroy of India *was the first of its kind on a P&O liner and designed in a distinctly Pompeian style by Inchcape's daughter Elsie.*

Above: The First Class Cabin-de-luxe on board Viceroy of India *was the height of luxury with an en suite bathroom and additional room for accompanying maids or valets.*

From the pale classicism of the Robert Adam-inspired First Class Reading and Writing room (right) to the baronial grandeur of the Smoking room (above), Viceroy's *interiors were luxurious by their aristocratic associations to stately homes ashore.*

Viscountess Inchcape (as she now was) continued to be involved in the design of the Company's ships this time with her eldest daughter, Lady Margaret Shaw, wife of Inchcape's successor in 1932, Alexander Shaw. Both women had a hand in P&O's latest liners, launched in the early 1930s for the Australian run. Inchcape decided that these ships should have Scottish place names, the first being *Strathnaver*, the title he himself had adopted on his elevation to the peerage in 1911. In the interiors of the early 'Straths', Viscountess Inchcape and Lady Margaret still clung affectionately to the 'historical', reflecting the style of their own Scottish baronial home, Glenapp Castle in Ayrshire.

In all other respects the 'Straths' broke with a number of long-held P&O traditions. They sported a bright white livery (replacing the traditional black) with buff funnels earning them the name the 'White Sisters'. And for the first time P&O provided more 'tourist' or second-class, than first-class accommodation, encouraging a new generation of passengers: *'The Tourist accommodation in certain of the Company's vessels provides an economic means of travel, and the support accorded shows that the provision of comfortable accommodation at a moderate price is appreciated.'*

Internally, the 'Straths' made real advances in passenger comfort, with 'forced ventilation' and running water in all first-class cabins. There were marked design concessions reflecting the growing enthusiasm for 'health and beauty' through exercise and the inclusion of the 'Straths' in P&O's summer cruising schedule. The swimming pools and the dance floors now had walls that could be folded back to provide open-air swimming and dancing and the sports decks were increasingly generous in size, said to be particularly appreciated by Australian passengers.

In hull and structure the third 'Strath' in the class, *Strathmore*, mirrored its stable mate on the Australia run, *Orion*, launched for the Orient Line in the same year. But there the similarities ended. The traditional interiors of *Strathmore*, at the hands of Waring & Gillow, epitomised the 'upholsterart' so scathingly dismissed by Sir Colin Anderson of the Orient Line. Anderson, together with the architect Brian O'Rorke, was leading the charge for a revolution in the interior design of liners:

'With the treatment by Mr. Brian O'Rorke of the new Orient liner, Orion, the paradox that a seafaring nation should prefer to deny the sea in its decorations has ceased to be. It now seems stranger than ever that Renaissance fireplaces, Louis Quinze lounges, Tudor dining-rooms, should ever have been thought

Opposite: Like the Viceroy of India *(top), the design of* Strathnaver's *interiors (bottom) still drew heavily on past historical styles (1938 Brochure).*

*By contrast ,*Orion *represented a modernist, functional approach to interior design: First Class Gallery (top); detail from Lynton Lamb's decorative panel in the Lounge (bottom).*

Stratheden *at anchor off Port Said. The painting was commissioned to commemorate the ship's launch and P&O's centenary in 1937. (Norman Wilkinson)*

suited to a ship, which, however luxurious, is no more respected by the elements than the veriest tramp.'
The Times, 17th August 1935

Anderson's belief that a ship was not so much a 'floating hotel' as a 'peculiarly mobile vehicle', was to influence the design of P&O ships in the post-war period leading up to the merger of the Orient Line and P&O (under the direction of his brother Sir Donald Anderson) in 1960.

In Britain's post-war revival of manufacturing industries and export trade, the importance of design was beginning to be appreciated. Not only did designers by then have an active professional body to represent their interests – the Society of Industrial Artists – but they were recognised at government level with the setting up of the Council of Industrial Design. And then came the joyous Festival of Britain, in 1951, which provided so many young designers with the opportunity to display their talents.

The Director of Architecture for the Festival was Sir Hugh Casson and it was to him that P&O turned in 1957 to lead the design team for their latest liner, *Canberra*, to be built and operated in parallel with the Orient Line's *Oriana*. Casson had some experience in the design of ships having worked on the Royal Yacht *Britannia*. He was a shipping enthusiast and perhaps held a sentimental attachment to the Company – his parents having met on a P&O voyage. Casson was given overall responsibility for the interior design of the ship and first-class accommodation, with John Wright designing the tourist-class public rooms and Barbara Oakley the cabins, walkways and crew accommodation. Wright had worked on the Festival of Britain and with Casson on *R.Y. Britannia*, whilst Oakley had already assisted P&O with the post-war liners *Arcadia* and *Iberia*.

Canberra presented her designers with a real opportunity for a ship to shape the future. Thanks to the intervention of P&O's young naval architect, John West, *Canberra* followed the tanker principle: her engines were placed aft leaving a clear central or midship section which allowed for generous public rooms and deck space above. With regards to interior design, Casson was a little unsure how 'modern' P&O was prepared to go. The Company's design statement had been a trifle ambiguous – a 'sharp break with all that is outdated' but nothing 'revolutionary'. Casson, perhaps to cover himself, suggested to Sir Donald Anderson that there should be a design sub-committee to guide him, to which Anderson replied:

'There is no one better fitted here than my brother Colin to give decisions on anything on which you want a ruling, and he will be glad to do so…. Colin will act for all of us in this matter.'
Sir Donald Anderson, 25th October 1960

Casson and (Colin) Anderson were well known to one another and shared an understanding of the basic design precepts that would govern *Canberra*:

'Ship interiors demand simple forms, clean surfaces, clear colours and good serviceable materials left to speak for themselves. Gimmicks quickly become tedious. The latest fashion is within a few months a yawning bore. Too many patterns, too many colours, too much art, too much diversity of character – all devised in well-meant endeavours to achieve 'interest' – defeat, in the end, their own object.'
Sir Hugh Casson, 1961

They sought to achieve 'the maximum of results by the minimum of means' a philosophy shared by John Wright, to whom Casson expressed his dislike of earlier conventions in liner design:

'The normal decorative devices – murals, bas-relief etched mirrors – or such straightforward fancy-dress resorts as Louis Seize or Tudor – have been overplayed in the last twenty years to such an extent that they are now hardly observed by the passengers.'
Sir Hugh Casson, 18th October 1960

In 1953 Casson had set up the first Interior Design course at the Royal College of Art in London and besides reflecting much of the gaiety and colour of the Festival of Britain, *Canberra* became something of a Royal College affair. Casson involved both college students and several of his academic colleagues. Robert Goodden, then Professor of Silversmithing and Jewellery, provided glass murals; Julian Trevelyan and his wife, Mary Fedden, both created murals, and the College's Fine Art tutor, Ruskin Spear, painted four life-size portraits for the 'Cricketer's Tavern'. David Hockney, then a student at the RCA, was given a free hand in the 'Pop Inn' (*Canberra's* teenage area) producing pokerwork 'sgraffiti' panels, which in turn would be overlaid with the graffiti of young passengers.

Colour was to be one of the distinguishing features of *Canberra's* interiors. The Bonito Club shimmered with shocking flame pinks and oranges, rich blue-green rubber floors covered the staircases and hallways and Barbara

Opposite: Canberra *emerging from the stocks at the Harland & Wolff shipyard in Belfast in 1960. (Harland & Wolff)*

Canberra. *First Class staircase (above) between the Meridian Room and Crow's Nest Observation Lounge (below) designed by Hugh Casson and Timothy Rendle.*

John Wright designed the Cricketers' Tavern (above) and the teenage Pop Inn
(below) with its graffiti panels by David Hockney. (Stewart Bale, May 1961)

'*Striking curtains and bedspreads in shocking pink, tangerine and amber on white make this Tourist Class cabin in light beech distinctly eye-catching. Pale grey bulkheads in stippled plastic blend with lavender and grey lino and the violet carpet...*'

ALMA BIRK, 1961

Colourful artists' impressions promoted Canberra *as a new and very different departure for P&O.*

Souvenir brochure produced for Canberra's maiden voyage.

John West was responsible for the overall design of Canberra, including the iconic funnels. West joined P&O as Assistant Naval Architect in 1952 rising to Assistant Manager for P&O Orient Management Ltd., by the time Canberra entered service. (April 1961)

Oakley's cabins were furnished with emerald green, amethyst, red and tangerine cushions and curtains.

'The seats of Ernest Race chairs, the coloured balls projecting at all angles, sections of wall, a ceiling, it was citrus sunshine all the way.' Ruth Artmonsky, 2010

Canberra's designers were unequivocally 'modern' in their use of new materials. Although fine hardwoods were still found in many of the first-class rooms, there was a proliferation of plastics, laminates, fibreglass, faux fabrics and fluorescents. The laminate, 'Perstorp', was particularly popular for use in public areas where it could be used decoratively with little or no ongoing maintenance required.

Canberra not only represented a total break with anything 'historic', but reflected the focus of P&O's passenger trade shifting from the Indian Ocean to Australasia. The choice of her name – an aboriginal term for 'meeting place' – and those of many of the public rooms on Canberra (Menzies Room, Pacific Restaurant, Island Room, Alice Springs Room) reflected the Company's long and close ties to Australia. And there were conscious Australasian touches in the ship's decoration, including a replica of a Maori war canoe and the Bonito murals, by Humphrey Spender, inspired by aboriginal symbols and drawings.

With three quarters of her berths allocated to tourist class and cosy six-berth cabins, Canberra could accommodate over 2,000 passengers and a crew of 900. She was designed on an ambitious scale sufficiently versatile to cater for P&O's traditional passengers together with a boom in emigration to Australia and a growing interest in cruising.

A boyhood cruise on the 'new' Canberra left a lasting impression:

'I was taken out of school a few days early in the summer of 1962 for a seven day cruise. The fare was £72 each, first class, for a week-long trip calling at Madeira and Gibraltar. I remember sneering at the one-class option on the seemingly ancient Strathmore and Stratheden (ventilated by the punkah louvre system – how positively medieval!), so we opted for the spanking new one.'

Whether Canberra actually was 'the ship to shape the future', as hype would have it, is arguable. But for P&O she marked both the end of an era of passenger liners and the start of a new class of ships, designed solely for comfort and the conventions of cruising.

Opposite: Canberra's striking radar mast photographed at night in 1961.

Above: Looking aft along Viceroy of India's *upper decks.*

Opposite: Ranpura's *upper decks captured in a dramatic night-time shot.*

'*If I had my time over again I would alter nothing. I would do exactly the same; I would go to sea in the P&O Company, hope to do my duty by my ship, and achieve at the last a command as good as the Himalaya; I could not wish for a better.*' Captain D. G. Baillie, 1957

CAPTAINS & CREWS

The Captain, or, in P&O terminology, the 'Commander', reigned supreme over all the crew. The Company's early Captains were usually drawn from the Royal Navy or from other established shipping lines such as from the Honourable East India Company's mercantile fleet. The P&O Captain's uniform was a navy-blue frock coat, double breasted with eight buttons in each row and half-inch straps of gold braid on each shoulder and three buttons on the cuff. A similar rig existed for officers – only the number of buttons, and the amount of gold, decreased as one came down the ranks in status.

The career of Captain James L. Dunkley is typical of a P&O Captain. Like so many in the Company, Dunkley began his training on board HMS *Worcester* (at the Thames Nautical Training College) and joined P&O as a cadet at the age of seventeen. When war was declared in 1939 he was second officer in *Rajputana* and, as a lieutenant RNR, he remained with the ship, in its new wartime role as an armed merchant cruiser escorting Atlantic convoys. In 1941 *Rajputana* was torpedoed by a German U-boat, 150 miles south of Iceland; Dunkley was one of the last officers to leave the sinking vessel. He continued to serve in the RNR, receiving an OBE for his devotion to duty, before returning to P&O in 1946 and taking his first command of the cargo ship *Surat* in 1955. His last command was *Canberra* and, in 1964, he was appointed Commodore of the P&O fleet, a position and honour which he held until 1968.

A P&O Captain tended to be viewed with awe, and surrounded by pomp and rituals. One Captain recalled the subservience required by protocol for carrying out the most routine task:

'*There was enormous dignity attached to a liner officer in those days. For instance, in the simple operation of drawing a little circle to mark the ship's noon position…I had a Quartermaster to assist me. He opened the frame and held the dividers for me…*' Captain Gordon Steele, reminiscing in 1957

The Captain, unfettered in the early years by telephone, telegram or radio, ruled his realm, including his passengers, with autocratic disdain. A certain individual was remembered for his particularly iron hand:

Opposite: Commodore Dunkley on the bridge of Canberra *c.1964.*

'Besides the foremastmen, stokers, coal trimmers and boys, there is:-

The Captain

A Chief Mate

2nd 3rd 4th Chief Mates

Boatswain

Mate

Native Boatswain

Mate

Carpenter

Mate

And other petty officers

TO NAVIGATE THE SHIP

A Purser, Purser's mate, or clerk

A Steward with about 12 servants

A Stewardess with assistant

Butcher and mate

Baker and mate

A professional Cook with many assistants

A Boots

A Storekeeper

A surgeon

FOR PASSENGERS

For the mails there is a naval officer on board...

A Chief Engineer

A Second, Third, Fourth and apprentices

A boilermaker'

FOR ENGINE ROOM

DIARY OF JAVA-BOUND ENGINEER, *ORIENTAL*, 22ND AUGUST 1846

P&O Engineers on the deck of Massilia, c.1884. The early uniform for engineers then was similar to deck officers, excepting the gold braid which was found on their caps only.

'His liner's discipline was a byword even outside the Company. It extended to the passengers. Every morning at eleven o'clock one would see a string of them lined up outside his cabin as defaulters for being late for meals or transgressing the ship's bounds. The strange thing was, the passengers liked it. It relieved the dullness of the voyage.'
Captain Gordon Steele, 1957

A young officer on board *Delta*, writing of his Captain, suggested that discipline was not merely a matter of individual eccentricity but at the core of P&O's shipboard mores:

'A formidable martinet, he set a fantastically high standard of discipline and smartness, even by the P&O yardstick. His strictness over one's neat appearance, such punctilio as the way one saluted, came on or off watch…or took charge of a gangway I could appreciate, for I was beginning to discern the tremendous tradition of efficiency fostered by the Company for close on eighty five years.'
Captain D.G. Baillie, reminiscing in 1957

Although, in later years, Captains were much sought after for their social cachet, their earlier counterparts were characterised as of rougher material. A passenger on the *Himalaya* to Singapore in 1854, writing home to his father, was less reverential:

'At dinner the Captain's health was proposed and he replied in a very neat speech — We made a terrible row in cheering him. He is a go-ahead fellow and not possessed of the 'suaviter in modo', but we must make great allowance for his arduous and trying position.'
William Adamson, *Himalaya*, 1st February 1854

One of the most appreciative tributes to a P&O Captain was penned by Thackeray, who dedicated the published account of his Mediterranean 'tour' to Captain Samuel Lewis of *Iberia* in 1844:

'After a voyage, during which the captain of the ship has displayed uncommon courage, seamanship and affability, or other good qualities, grateful passengers often present him with a token of their esteem, in the shape of teapots, tankards, trays, etc., of precious metals. Among authors, however, bullion is a much rarer commodity than paper, whereof I beg you to accept a little in the shape of this small volume.'
William Makepeace Thackeray, 24th December 1845

Captain J.B. Browning and Senior Officers photographed in their full dress "whites" on board Maloja, *January 1930.*

Beneath the Captain were his Chief Mates and other officers who could also be called upon for social duties; although a directive from Sir Thomas Sutherland suggests there was some concern as to how these duties were conducted:

'On board some of the Company's steamers we fear that there is too much laxity permitted to the officers in associating with passengers. Courtesy and politeness to passengers are essential but there is no necessity for carrying this to the point of intimacy.'
P&O Circular, August 1872

Another concern for Head Office was the relationship between the Captain and his senior deck officers and the Chief Engineer and his department, who were, not infrequently, at loggerheads over the speed of the ship. For the Captain, strict adherence to the mail schedule was paramount (there were penalties for lateness), whilst the Chief Engineer was naturally more concerned with coal supplies and the maintenance of his machinery. In the days of sail a Captain could feel secure in his grasp of everything involved, but, when it came to steamers, he was altogether more vulnerable and disadvantaged by his limited technical knowledge. The tensions did not go unnoticed:

'Complaints have been made that for some reason there seems to have been a sort of antagonistic feeling between engineers and officers which has been very hurtful to the Company's interests…there are some Chief Engineers who seem to consider themselves sole masters of their departments, responsible only to their Superintendent Engineers, and perfectly independent of everyone else. If such ideas exist, they must be at once abandoned. It is important that perfect confidence should exist between the engine and deck departments.'
P&O Instructions for Chief Engineers, 1867

The Captain could also, on occasion, be challenged by the Admiralty Officer, sent out to accompany the mail. The mail contracts stipulated that the Admiralty Officer enjoyed:

'…full authority in all cases to require due and strict execution of this contract on the part of the said Company, and to determine every question whenever arising, relative to proceeding to sea, or putting into harbour, or to the necessity of stopping to assist any vessel in distress, or to save human life; and the decision of such officer as aforesaid shall in each and every such case be final and binding on the said Company…'
Mail Contract, 1853

ONE OF THE NATIVE CREW. MORNING NOON AND NIGHT THEY COULD BE SEEN POLISHING AND CLEANING.

"ROWLY OTHERWISE MISS ROWLANDS OUR VERY CAPABLE STEWARDESS.

Some of the crew of Moldavia *captured in a souvenir album of photographs taken in 1935. (Martins).*

Thackeray, nevertheless, paints a more than sympathetic picture of one, Lieutenant Bundy, the Admiralty Officer on P&O's *Oriental*:

'He is a very well-educated man and reads prodigiously…. He is not in the least angry at his want of luck in the profession…So he carries her Majesty's mails meekly through this world, waits upon port-admirals and captains in his old glazed hat, and is as proud of the pennon at the bow of his little boat, as if it were flying from the mainmast of a thundering man-of-war.'
William Makepeace Thackeray, 1846

There was little doubt that the mail and its schedule took precedence on any voyage, often at the expense of passengers and freight; both could be left behind if not on board by the time the mail was due to depart.

The purser was vital to passengers' welfare, responsible not only for the ship's supply of food and drink, but also for furnishings and linen, crockery and cutlery, and almost everything else on board, save the actual running of the ship. The purser was beholden to two masters:

'As Purser you will have two objects constantly before you, the one being to give satisfaction in the highest possible degree to passengers, and the other to maintain the strictest economy in your department. Experience has shown that these two important objects may, by proper management, be both secured at one and the same time.'
P&O Instructions for Pursers, Clerks and Stewards, 1860

The daily round of the purser is humorously described in a log of *Bendigo* published in 1924:

'The 'wet nurse' of every ship is the Purser. He it is who has to listen to all complaints concerning the inner workings of the catering department, to listen to the hundred and one senseless questions asked by the unsophisticated, and he it is also who takes care not only of our persons but of our purses.'
W. North White, 1924

The cabin stewards and stewardesses inevitably tended to build the closest relationships with passengers and were, invariably, praised for carrying out their daily duties and for the help they gave to those in distress. A young woman, Lena Bigsby, marvelled at her stewardess coping with sea-sickness in the Bay of Biscay:

'…dinner — we met our Goanese Table Steward, by name Amos & his reply to any request was 'I get it', and he did, every time.'

MRS M. A. WATTS, *ARCADIA*, 16TH MARCH 1963

ON THE RIGHT IS KRASTO OR BISTO AS WE CALLED HIM OUR NOT SO CAPABLE STEWARD

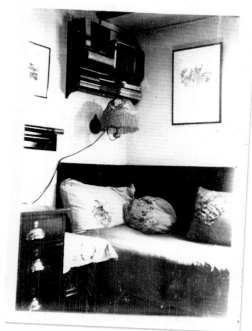

SERANG & SECUNNIES

More than any other archives, personal diaries, letters and photo albums offer the most immediate glimpse into the past. For Company crew, the weeks and months at sea spawned life-long friendships and albums filled with nicknames and favourite poses. In addition to the regular crew, P&O had always employed a ship's surgeon or doctor and in time, medical facilities and staff expanded to include nurses. Selected photographs from 1914 to 1967 in the P&O Heritage Collection, including the albums of Commodore Dunkley.

The weekly inspection of crew took place every Sunday before church service.
The carpenter and bosun head up the line in Harry Furniss' comic sketch from 1898.

'*The poor stewardess had 16 ladies in bed all day, having to take all their meals to them, it's wonderful how good-natured & bright she kept all day.*'
Lena Bigsby, *Macedonia*, c.1910

Whilst a journalist (on a P&O tanker no less) waxed poetic about the competence of his steward: '*…when returning to my cabin from the cinema, I found myself regarding the steward's scrupulous preparation of the room for the night; superb P&O butlering, with the curtains drawn, the quilt turned back and the pillows fluffed, all the day's paraphernalia sorted out and put away or neatly arranged, thermos of iced water beside the bed, a bowl of fruit, the overhead lights turned off and only the reading light by the bed casting a gentle confined glow.*'
Noël Mostert, *Ardshiel*, 1976

Of all the crew to feature in diaries and letters home, almost without exception, the greatest comment was reserved for the Asian crews:

'*The crew are mustered in clean clothes and inspected by the Commander every Sunday, and this is quite a sight to be remembered when the whole of the crew, European and native with the exception of a few immediately engaged in the navigation of the ship, turn out in their 'Sunday best' and 'toe the line' on the upper decks. The Lascars and the firemen in their clean white coats with gorgeous turbans and multi-coloured kumberbunds, and the seedie boys in their display of elaborately embroidered silk waist coats, form a picturesque study, and it is only on such an occasion that the casual traveller recognises the number and variety of men that are required for the equipment of a First Class Mail Steamer in all its departments.*'
George Henderson, *Rome*, 1901

In any one ship a variety of languages could be heard, including Gujarati, Malay, Pushtu, Bengali, Hindustani or Portuguese. Depending on their duties on board (deck, engine, cook, steward), Asian crews tended to originate from the same areas and villages where they shared the same religion, diet and general culture. The Kalasis, or seamen, came mainly from the coastal regions of Malabar and the Portuguese colony of Daman (and the adjacent areas). As they 'signed their articles' in Bombay, the Kalasis were known generally as the 'Bombay crews' and were a mix of Hindus and Muslims.

'*It is the Kalasis who heave on ropes and scrub decks, who preserve the ship against the inroads of weather and time by*

'*Asian seamen keep the ship spick and span, polishing, painting and scrubbing the decks long before the passengers rise in the mornings…. Their ready smile and colourful uniform are now truly a part of the P&O way of life.*'

MEN OF THE SHIPS, 1960

One of the many and much-valued Asian seamen on board Arcadia *photographed in 1956. (W. A. Fortens).*

chipping and scraping, painting and varnishing; they overhaul the cargo, the cargo blocks and gears and, in a phrase, keep everything looking "shipshape and Bristol fashion".'
M. Watkin-Thomas, September 1955

The Agwalas, or firemen, who made up the largest group on board after the seamen, came traditionally from the Mardan district (Pakistan) and Kashmir and were Muslim. The stewards tended to be Goan and were devout Roman Catholics with Portuguese names. Both the firemen and the stewards were supervised by their own Serang, and his assistants, the Tindals. The Serangs in turn reported to the chief officer and were responsible for work standards.

The different customs, food, music and clothing of the Asian crew were a constant fascination to passengers leaving Britain and the Mediterranean for the first time. The Kalasis were particularly resplendent in blue embroidered, knee-length tunics (lachis), a red folded sash (rhumai) round their waists, white pantaloons and a topi on their heads. The Serangs and Tindals could be

distinguished by the kind of ribbon they sported on their topis and by the boatswain pipes, hung on a silver chain around their necks. The Asian crews would eat separately, mainly curries and rice, and, when in port, would play their own instruments and music.

Invariably, officers reported preferring Asian to European crews, who were more conscientious in their work, courteous in their behaviour and could be relied on *not* to drink alcohol. In 1866 the Asian crew made up over half of P&O's total crew afloat. Over time, whole families and generations joined P&O to form an essential part of the Company:

'In its long and eventful history, the P&O Company has been fruitfully served by many devoted servants. Not least among them should be numbered the countless thousands comprising Asian crews…Generations of them have come from their humble homes, all over the sub-continent, each to devote the best part of a lifetime to serve in the Company's ships. In the P&O…they have become an institution.'
M. Watkin-Thomas, September 1955

For passengers there was little to do but relax, particularly in warm weather, but for the crew there was always work to be done. (W. W. Lloyd, 1892).

A specially designed altar in the mess on board Canberra *gave the Goanese crew a place to worship. (Willoughby Gullachesen).*

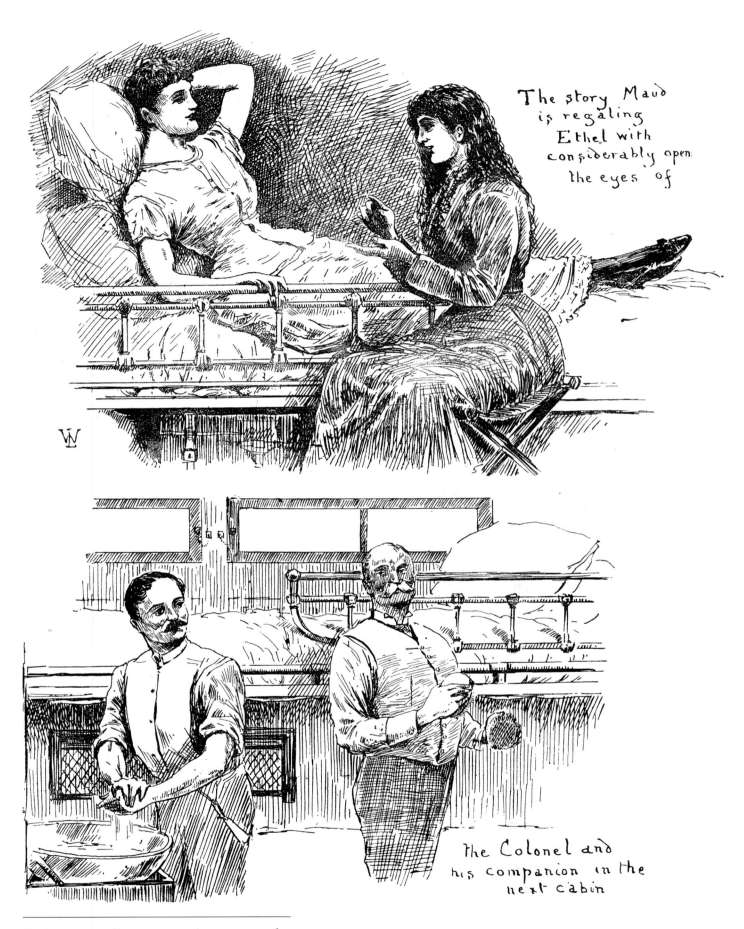

The story Maud
is regaling
Ethel with
considerably open
the eyes of

The Colonel and
his companion in the
next cabin

Close living quarters and long voyages meant that passengers were often forced to get to know each other rather well. (W. W. Lloyd, 1892)

TRAVELLING TYPES

'P&O liners carry England in her sons and daughters and her commerce to the ends of the earth.'
Rt. Reverend, G. Vernon Smith, 14th October 1937

From the very beginning, P&O carried people to the Empire for work or pleasure but mostly the former. An early passenger's account for *Hindostan* in 1842 gives a typical cross section of those travelling P&O: a Colonel returning from furlough, a Lieutenant going out to join the Third Light Dragoons, Mr Church (a merchant), Mr Derrer (going out to join P&O in Calcutta), cadets for the Indian army, Indian civil servants, a Reverend going out to the Church Missionary Society in Madras, a teacher for Vepery Grammar School, a coffee and a sugar planter, a doctor, a lawyer, several young men seeking work in India, and, rather curiously described, some writers *'of whom I saw very little'*.

Some fifty years later the mix was much the same:

'All was hurry, scurry, and confusion. Officers, civil and military, returning to duty; wives and families going out for the "cold season"; MPs alive to their responsibilities as "members for India" bent on visiting their distant constituency; business men going to sell their wares, or to buy tea or jute or indigo; the inevitable army of globetrotters; missionaries filled with noble purpose; youths redolent of confidence and hope, going to fight for fame and fortune; and perhaps most interesting of all, fair maidens speeding at the call of love, braving even the blastful Bay of Biscay, to be led…to the altar under the burning sun of India. Add to this concourse a full quota of returning natives, Parsees and Mohammedans as well as Hindus, and then but an imperfect summary of the gathering is obtained…'
Fred Reynolds, *India*, 1896

The 'fair maidens speeding' came to be known as the 'fishing fleet', some travelling with fish already on their baits, others in hope, some said to be so optimistic of their chances as to have brought their trousseau with them. One young girl, travelling on the *Macedonia*, wrote baldly home to her mother of her pique at being placed at a table next to a poor specimen when other girls were getting to know much nicer men. However, the odds were still stacked in her favour:

'Already I've spoken to more men in ten days, than possible during six weeks, or even six months in Southboro…'
Lena Bigsby, *Macedonia*, c.1910

'It is so hot that even the young ladies have ceased to flirt, and languidly fan themselves under double awnings and waving punkahs.'

EDWIN ARNOLD, *PARRAMATTA*, 1886

The Ananias of the Smoking room.

The young man Globe Trotting at his parent's expense

The Missionary going to China

a Naval Officer

The Subaltern returning from leave

A successful Colonist.

Two little New Zealanders.

The man who talks a great deal of yachting "shop" & collapses at the first breeze of wind.

A Yankee Wanderer. (our pianist)

The Schoolboy who makes it hot for the gul with a catapu

A broad spectrum of society frequented P&O steamers. Military and government officials travelled in great numbers and enjoyed a subsidised fare creating, in the early days of first class only, an unofficial second class. (Detail from an original sketch in pen and ink by W.W. Lloyd, 1892).

The victim of mal de mer who lives on smelling salts

One of our Flirts

Thumbnail sketch of the Commander

Quiet but dangerous

For Melbourne.

Two of the Captain's "Wards"

Our Foghorns (automatic)

The least troublesome passenger in the ship.

A grass "Widdy"

A West Ender bound for Shepheard's & the Nile

*'The Australian run...
was indisputably the
voyage par excellence for
pretty young women, who
far outnumbered the men
on the passenger-list of
every Sydney ship.'*

CAPTAIN D. G. BAILLIE, 1957

*The 1930s era epitomised the romance and glamour of travel by sea. From advertisements
(above, 1933), to the real thing on board the deck of* Viceroy of India *(right).*

The Australian route seems to have been particularly frequented by eligible young ladies, often girls being sent to Europe to complete their education: *'trimming their "crepe de Chine" sails for Colombo and points north at the right season of the year'*.

Many of the men travelling on P&O steamers were in the Services and bound for their regiments and bases in India. In times of emergency or war the Government could, and did, requisition part of the Company's fleet for troop transport and hospital ships. With a widespread fleet, and an established infrastructure, P&O could respond rapidly to the call of duty.

In the early 1830s, before the establishment of P&O, Willcox and Anderson provided ships and assistance in the insurrections in Spain and Portugal. By the mid-nineteenth century, when the Admiralty found itself with an ageing fleet, the Company's steamers could be relied on for trooping. In the Crimea, P&O ships not only transported the troops but also their horses and armaments and Florence Nightingale with her nurses out on their way to Scutari.

The P&O fleet had always carried its own cannons and arms with which to protect the mails and to defend the Company's routes, particularly in the pirate-ridden seas of the Far East. When the 'Jubilee' ships were built in the 1880s, they had gun platforms already in place, which made them easily converted when required. P&O ships played a part in the Boxer Rebellion of 1900 and the Boer War (1899-1902), but it was only with the outbreak of the First World War that the Company was seriously involved, with some two-thirds of the fleet requisitioned for war service. Not only were P&O ships carrying troops but its own volunteer crews, who returned to the Company's service after the cessation of hostilities. Again in the Second World War, P&O ships were to be found on convoy and patrol duties, as hospital ships and ferrying troops across the world:

'We saw hundreds upon hundreds of soldiers and knew there were thousands below decks.'
Mrs D. Asher, *Strathallan*, 1942

The last, and least expected, tour of duty saw P&O ships once more carrying troops and essential equipment, requisitioned this time to serve in the Falkland Islands. Four Company ships, *Canberra*, *Uganda*, *Norland* and *Elk*, together with their volunteer crews survived the conflict unscathed, returning to rapturous homecomings.

In the days of the Empire, no P&O passenger list was

'It is doubtful if ever before, in peace or war, combat troops had been transported in luxury equal to that we enjoyed aboard the Strathnaver.'

SOLDIER IN 2/4TH INFANTRY BATTALION, REMINISCING IN 1950

Opposite: On 10th January 1940 Strathnaver, *carrying the Second Australian Imperial Force into war, left Sydney supposedly in secret; the families of the troops had other ideas.*

Rapid deployment practice on board Canberra *bound for the Falklands, April 1982.* Canberra *carried three helicopters and over 2,500 troops. (Ministry of Defence).*

'*All through this trying and anxious time they have displayed the greatest gallantry and they have never uttered a murmur. The war has made heavy inroads on our officers and engineers, and all who could be spared have joined the forces…*'

LORD INCHCAPE, 13TH DECEMBER 1916

Survivors from the Battle of Jutland on board P&O's Plassy,
which served as a hospital ship during the First World War.

complete without a sprinkling of missionaries, travelling at a specially reduced rate and carrying their particular 'Word' out to India and beyond.

'Miss Anson feels much indebted to the Company for their liberality in allowing her to travel for the third time in five years with the reductions allowed to missionaries, of which she has very thankfully availed herself, being an hon. missionary of the Ladies Association in connection with the Society for the Propagation of the Gospel.'
Miss Anson, 1890s

Some missionaries appear to have gone outwards with such fervour that they began their work whilst still on board:

'We have a Jesuit and an Episcopalian clergyman on board – with the latter I have had a discussion and he laboured to prove that the Church of England was in a direct line of descent from the Apostles.'
William Adamson, *Himalaya*, 7th February 1854

GENERAL VISCOUNT KITCHENER, G.C.B., G.C.M.G.
"He hath a wisdom that doth guide his valour."—*Shakespeare.*
Raphael Tuck & Sons' "Empire" Postcard. Series 839.

Postcard of General Kitchener dated 1902 and sent from London to Singapore via three different Company vessels. Kitchener travelled by P&O in 1911.

Pilgrims were also carried by P&O, whether on their way to Mecca or Jerusalem, and special arrangements would be made for different dietary needs and food preparation not only for the crews but for pilgrim passengers too:

'…there are perfect arrangements whereby a high-caste Hindu and an orthodox Mohammedan may keep his caste and religion while on board the steamer.'
Anonymous passenger, *Pekin*, 1891

As Sir Thomas Sutherland was once heard to lament in a lean period; *'we have no American millionaires like my friends of the Cunard Company travelling in our ships or if they ever travel in our vessels they travel incognito and save their money'.* Nevertheless the Company had plenty of its own 'great and good' who travelled P&O:

'Bombay ships in those days certainly carried a great many interesting and important people: Governors of Presidencies or Provinces of India; Maharajahs and their enormous retinues… famous figures in politics or society going out to enjoy what was then a fashionable and popular winter pastime of the wealthy – a Cold Weather in India. From October to December the outward-bound ships would be packed with – in the main – the well-dressed and the well-bred, the socially impeccable: the type of person who inspired the phrase: "They met disaster with the icy calm of the P&O first-class passenger".'
Captain D. G. Baillie, reminiscing in 1957

Among many, Lord Curzon, Lord Elgin and Viscount General Kitchener all arrived to take up their Empire posts on P&O – Kitchener making few appearances on the promenade deck for: *'fear of being buttonholed by the Ladies'.* As India took her first steps towards independence it was a P&O ship that brought the First Commission, including Clement Attlee and Lord Strathcona, to the talks in 1928. And it was on 29th August 1931 that a small, slightly-built, barely dressed man on a mission – Mahatma Gandhi – travelled on *Rajputana* to London for the Round Table Conference on Independence.

Besides the Viceroys, and the diplomats, there were cricket teams bound for Australia and India, mountaineers with Everest in their sights and explorers, among them Dr Livingstone, all aboard P&O. There were writers too, the earliest of any note being Thackeray who penned his appreciation:

'With what a number of sights and pictures – of novel and delightful remembrances, does a man furnish his mind after

Mahatma Gandhi pictured with Captain H. M. Jack, Master of Rajputana *during Gandhi's voyage from Bombay in 1931.*

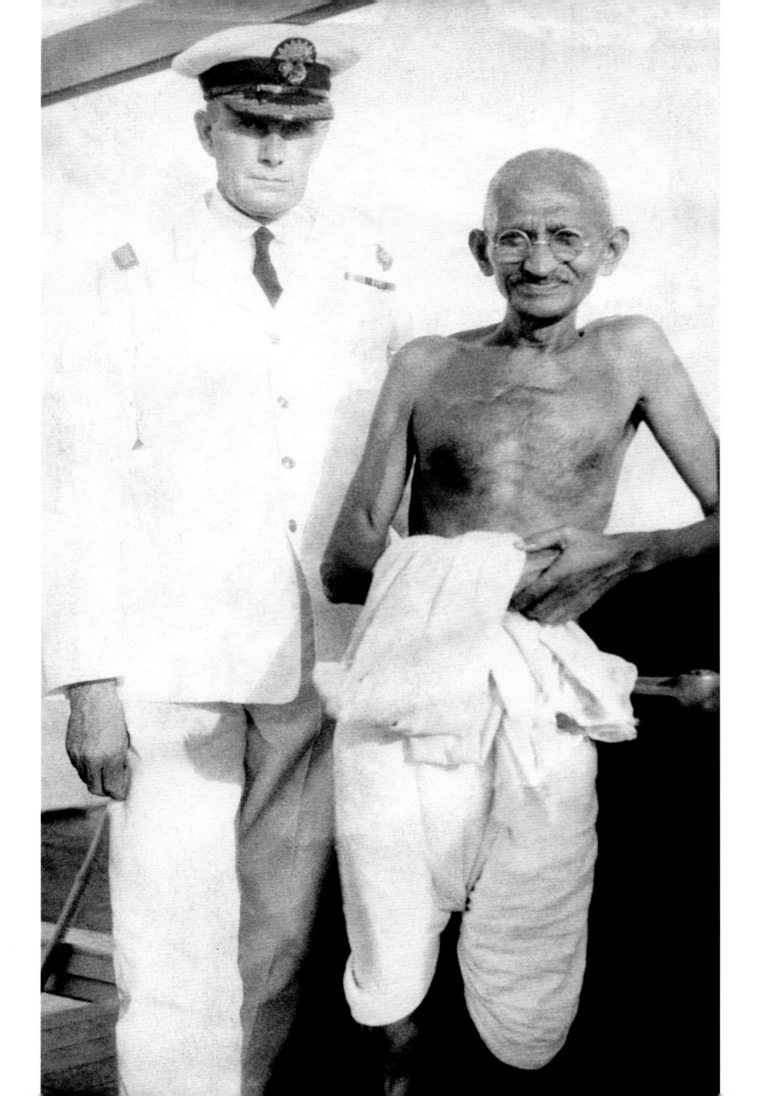

'Lines of chairs on the promenade deck,

Smell of engine room rising through hatches,

Mrs Blake, with a sunburnt neck,

Organizing Shuffleboard matches,

Missionaries with pale, kind eyes,

Drained of colour by savage skies,

Strumming militantly glum

Hymns on a harmonium.

Flying fish from the bow waves skittering,

Mrs Frobisher's endless tittering

And at night the great stars glittering'

NOËL COWARD, *P. & O.* 1930

Opposite: Illustration from a 1934 brochure for Strathnaver *and* Strathaird.

such a tour!… I forget what sea-sickness is now; though it occupies a woeful portion of my Journal. There was a time on board when the bitter ale was decidedly muddy; and the cook of the ship deserting in Constantinople, it must be confessed his successor was some time before he got his hand in. These sorrows have passed away with the soothing influence of time; the pleasures of the voyage remain, let us hope, as long as a life will endure…But the happiest and best of all the recollections, perhaps, are those of the hours passed at night on the deck, when the stars were shining overhead, and the hours were tolled at their time, and your thoughts were fixed on home far away.'
William Makepeace Thackeray, 1846

Charles Dickens travelled with Wilkie Collins and 'A. N. Other' from Genoa to Naples, on *Valetta* in 1853, and recounted the trials of sleeping on deck – 'no mattress, no blankets, nothing'; and of how he managed to secure a cabin for the three of them, and a good supply of food. For Mark Twain the experience was rather more enriching and educational:

'In the Oceana *the passengers dress for dinner – proof that it is the habit of the Indian Ocean to be smooth. I have never seen the custom before at sea, though I knew it existed in these*

Books were not only read but written on board, often inspired by the experience of the voyage itself. (Harry Furniss, 1898).

latitudes. Beautiful dresses, low necks, vivid colours…officers in uniform at the head of each table, electric light, richly decorated dining saloon – why, it looks like a swell banquet.'
Mark Twain, *Oceana*, January 1896

For a period Kipling travelled to and fro on P&O, homesick for the India where he had been born and where he could be away from what he saw as the dreariness and dampness of England. In his lengthy poem – *The Exiles' Line* – he not only catches the feeling of being an expat but the experience of travelling under the 'Quartered Flag' – the grimed stoker, the white decks, the gasping of the screw blades, and the 'great one upon the quarter deck, brow-bound with gold.'

'But we, the gypsies of the East, but we
Waifs of the land and wastrels of the sea
Come nearer home beneath the Quartered Flag
Than ever home shall come to such as we.'
Rudyard Kipling, 1890

It was Kipling who, in a letter to the publisher, Charles Scribner, in 1932, described Inchcape's last days aboard his private yacht:

'Out in the baby harbour lies a big yacht – almost a small liner – which belongs to Lord Inchcape, head of the P&O. She has been there over a week now. He is down with a bad chill. Nothing seems to move on her, except, now and then, a uniformed nurse.'
Rudyard Kipling, 21st March 1932

Although Somerset Maugham had none of the 'Empire' associations of Kipling, he travelled to the Far East a number of times during the 1920s to gather material for his books. His short story, *P&O*, written in 1923 describes the eventful homeward journey of Mrs Hamlyn – the arrival of a rag-tag of passengers at Singapore, the noisy bustle of departing from the harbour, the early mornings on deck, and so forth. Noël Coward turned to verse to capture the rhythm and humour of life at sea in *P. & O. 1930,* and Jules Verne used the Company's steamers to propel his famous fictional globetrotter, Phileas Fogg, around the world in eighty days in 1873.

Slow or fast, the experience of travelling P&O remained strongly in passengers' memories. Some fifty years after he himself had travelled as a boy from his native Ceylon, to attend school in South London, in 1954, Michael Ondaatje, in his novel *The Cat's Table*, sent his characters to England aboard the very same liner, *Oronsay*:

Medina, as a Royal yacht, leaving Portsmouth for Delhi in 1911. Many alterations were required internally and Medina had to have an extra mast borrowed from another P&O liner.

"We seem to be at the cat's table", the woman called Miss Lasqueti said, *"We're in the least privileged place"*. *It was clear we were located far from the Captain's Table, which was at the opposite end of the dining room.'*
Michael Ondaatje, 2011

It was anything but 'the cat's table' for visiting Royals. In 1849, at Prince Albert's suggestion, the Chairman and Managing Directors of P&O were delighted by the arrival of Queen Victoria and the Prince on board *Hindostan*, which was conveniently anchored close to Osborne House on the Isle of Wight. It was the start of the Company's royal connections. Forty years later the Queen's son, Prince Albert Victor, travelled to India on the *Oceana*. The *Evening Standard* announced in 1889:

'*The Peninsular and Oriental Company have made elaborate arrangements for Prince Albert Victor's voyage to India in their Steamship* Oceana. *Several state cabins have been thrown into three rooms for the Prince's use, and are elegantly decorated and upholstered. By the Prince's desire no change is to be made on deck, and the Prince, with his suite and a few select guests, will mess with the Captain in the Saloon.'*
Evening Standard, 11th October 1889

In 1911 P&O's newest liner *Medina* was completed and fitted as a Royal yacht for King George V and Queen Mary to travel to the Coronation Durbar at Delhi and to tour India. Another 'M' class, *Maloja*, was made available for visiting dignitaries and passengers wishing to follow the full programme of events, state dinners and receptions.

In the same year Princess Louise, the Princess Royal, with the Duke of Fife and their children, were travelling to Egypt on P&O's *Delhi*, when it was wrecked near Tangiers in a gale. The Royal party were rescued in good time but it was an unfortunate episode, and there were some who suggested that the Duke's death a year later (from ill-health) was linked to the disastrous voyage.

In 1935 the then Duchess of York (the late Queen Mother) launched *Strathmore* in Barrow-in-Furness (the Duchess being the daughter of the Earl of Strathmore). It was the first of many such occasions in which P&O ships, from liners and cruise ships to ferries, enjoyed a Royal naming.

In the early days the Company's steamers were strictly first class only, before gradually including a second class. In a new departure, in 1910 P&O started to carry emigrants and third-class passengers to Australia, using the slow route via the Cape.

King George V and Queen Mary photographed watching the games below on the deck of Medina

'We learnt next day that Dame Edith Sitwell was on board, but she stayed in her cabin all the time. I recognized Richard Gordon, author of 'Dr at Sea' etc. So that's how he gets his material!'

MRS M. A. WATTS, *ARCADIA*, 1963

Above: Captain Dunkley and Mrs McGuire on the bridge of Canberra, *1964.*

Opposite: P&O carried few of the Hollywood and film stars who frequented the transatlantic routes, but the ships themselves featured in a handful of films from Diamonds are Forever *to* Gandhi. *(Photograph: filming on board* Canberra *in 1965)*

'*We are getting near Aden now and will have to change there tomorrow into the Moldavia. There are very few passengers, mostly all men. I am wondering what the Australians will be like. Hope they are decent.*'

L. DYER, 31ST MARCH 1914

The Kemptons, on board Balranald, *leaving Australia after three years, unlike the majority of emigrants who stayed. Between 1947 and 1959, 360,000 people took up the assisted passage scheme and emigrated to Australia.*

The Company had bought the fleet of Lund's Blue Anchor Line and set about renaming the existing service, the P&O Branch Service, and ordering new 'B' class ships. *Bendigo*, in 1924, is recorded as making special facilities for a Salvation Army party of some 180 people being taken to Australia for what was clearly considered to be their betterment – some fifty-seven boys to work the land, some forty-two girls as home helps, three 'blue-eyed boys' for adoption, and some men and women to be put in hostels until work could be found for them.

After the Second World War, Australia was looking urgently to build up their labour force and P&O started to carry out optimistic emigrants on the Australian Government's scheme for what became known as the 'Ten Pound Poms'. The scheme ran from 1945 to 1973 and made a steady, if modest, contribution to P&O's turnover.

Another source of income was introduced in the early 1960s when BI began a programme of educational cruises, with up to 1,200 school children aboard per cruise, using the former troopships *Dunera*, *Devonia* and later *Nevasa*. The first two of these were old ships requiring expensive maintenance and it was decided to make a thorough conversion of BI's *Uganda* to replace them. Cabins were converted to dormitories, public rooms to classrooms, and deck space expanded for sports; stewardesses were renamed matrons, and teachers became party leaders. *Uganda* carried school children from 1968 to 1982, with summer cruises in the Western Mediterranean, the Atlantic and Scandinavia, and winter ones in the Eastern Mediterranean. Although BI was fully absorbed into P&O in 1971, *Nevasa* and *Uganda* were allowed to keep their BI livery. The *Uganda* was affectionately given nicknames by the children, such as 'Ug Tug' and 'Slave Ship *Uganda*' and diaries and logs (which seem to have been a compulsory part of life aboard) were full of the exotic excursions made from the ship to the Pyramids, Jerusalem, the Parthenon, Lanzarote's volcanoes and the like.

Cruising programmes for adults, which P&O had started with the *Vectis* in 1904, increased gradually over the years, with many of its passenger ships being used for seasonal cruising during the traditional off-peak periods for line voyages. The introduction of statutory paid holidays in 1936 doubtless contributed to the growth of cruises, but marketing made them not only desirable, but aspirational – 'I've just come back from a cruise' gave one an immediate 'peg up' and social kudos.

With the end of line voyages in 1974, P&O passenger liners were destined to become one-class cruise ships. Only P&O Ferries could now claim to run scheduled liner services across to Europe. Those who needed to travel had taken to the skies leaving only the leisured classes to while away the hours at sea.

For fourteen years Uganda *was a school at sea for thousands of children until its school days were cut short in April 1982 by the Falklands Conflict. (Coventry Evening Telegraph).*

Life on board sketched by William Lionel Wyllie on the deck of Peshawur *at sea.*

'A voyage to Australia is a large undertaking for most people, even in these days. After the first few days at sea the novelty of ship life begins to grow stale, and for many, time hangs heavily on the hands of those who are used to a busy life ashore. Therefore we must find amusements amongst ourselves.'
Captain G. H. Furlong, *Bendigo*, 1924

EATING AND DRINKING

Fighting boredom seems to have been the main preoccupation of travellers on board ship, although attending to the basics of life from washing and dressing to eating and drinking occupied a surprisingly large amount of time. From the earliest days of P&O the rhythm of shipboard life revolved around food and drink, which was served at least half a dozen times a day:

'The Bugle sounds at half past 8 o'clock, when most of us rise and dress, at 9 we breakfast – on the tea or coffee, hot rolls and hot and cold meat, fowls or anything we may fancy, at 12 we have luncheon of bread and cheese and butter washed down with wine, spirits or Ale – at 4 we dine, when we have soup, various kinds of roasts, fowls too, pastry, puddings and other light things in that line – cheese and celery – desert consisting of Apples, Oranges, Dried Fruit.'
William Adamson, *Himalaya*, 23rd January 1854

This was followed at 6pm by 'tea, coffee, biscuits, bread and butter' and 'grog and biscuits from eight till ten at night'. P&O's policy with regard to victualling was set out in one of several 'Instructions to Pursers' in 1860:

'The intention of the Company is that the fare should be plain but of the best quality of its kind with good sound wines. The greatest pains are taken by the Company to provide the table in a way that may give general satisfaction and the prices paid by the Company are liberal.'
P&O Instructions for Pursers, Clerks and Stewards, 1860

Whilst fresh vegetables were scarce, owing to the lack of refrigeration, everything else including wine and beers was provided in plentiful supply sometimes overwhelmingly so, as Captain Philip Colomb RN discovered in 1868:

'I dreaded the sound of the bell when I first heard it, and I dread the thought of it now. It began at 9.00 a.m. when you fell to at a strong breakfast. At noon you were rung to lunch, just heavy enough to spoil your appetite for dinner, whose knell sounded at 3.00. At 6.00 the bell attacked you for tea; and if it left you alone to take or avoid 'biscuits and grog' at 9.00 it was probably because your digestion was thought to be pretty well done up by that time. Those who have not travelled P&O will say, "How very weak of you to be commanded by the bell to eat when you knew it was not good for you!" Those who have so travelled will not make such a remark.'
Captain Philip Colomb, RN, 1868

A century of improvements in ship design transformed life on board from a test of fortitude to a pleasurable journey of choice. (Detail from Gala Night Menu, 1933)

With the introduction of refrigeration in the 1880s the carrying of livestock had ceased. This was a great saving in space on board but a glance at the contents of *Britannia*'s new refrigeration chambers suggests that there was no reduction in the amount of food on offer:

'30,000 lb fresh meat
3000 head of poultry
5000 lb fresh fish
500 lb fresh butter
850 lb Danish butter
800 gallons fresh milk in tins
2000 tins of condensed milk
40,000 eggs'
Scarborough Gazette, Britannia, 9th February 1888

With further refinements came welcome delicacies such as ice cream:

'…ices every night after dinner…I never tasted such delights in my life. A cream ice with iced damson juice over it was food fit for the gods….'
Lena Bigsby, *Macedonia*, c. 1910

P&O, unlike other lines, initially included drink in the price of their passage ticket. This would include not only beer, but spirits, good wines, aerated water and, twice a week, champagne. Passengers did not hold back and there are plentiful examples of Captains having to take heavy imbibers to task:

'The Captain was swearing away at a good rate this morning and blowing up two passengers who had got drunk and disturbed the passengers in their berths. He vowed to report them at Head Quarters (they were young fellows – one in the Queen's and the other in the Co's service) on arrival, and if they continued to misbehave he threatened to confine them to their cabins under the guard of a sentry.'
William Adamson, *Himalaya*, 27th January 1854

Above: Despite the primitive facilities, the choice and quantity of food in the early years was quite bewildering. (Menu dated 1865 and P&O china dating from 1840)

Opposite: The First Class Dining Saloon on board Medina *c. 1912, set up for dinner (with decorative silver-plate water jugs designed by Christopher Dresser).*

At the other extreme some passengers began to realise that one paid a higher fare for such a liberal supply of alcohol. Recalling the first voyage of *Hindostan* in 1842, Sir William Twynam wrote with some indignation of the injustice of the early arrangement:

'...*of issuing wines, beer, spirits and aerated waters free of cost to those making use of them, whilst all, including abstainers and moderate drinkers had to pay equally high rates of passage to cover the cost of liquor supplied free which must have been heavy.*'
Sir William Twynam, 1916

In the straitened times immediately following the opening of the Suez Canal, the Company decided to charge for drinks and lower the cost of fares accordingly. Bars then began to appear on P&O ships with strict regulations as to their usage:

'*At sea when passengers are aboard the bar will open between 8.00 a.m. and 9.00 a.m., 11.00 a.m. and 1.00 p.m., 3.00 p.m. and 9.30 p.m... No person will be allowed to drink at the bar, nor will liquors be allowed on deck except in case of sickness....*'
P&O Circular, January 1871

It might be thought that consumption would fall with the introduction of charges for alcohol, but the stores loaded on to *Britannia* in the 1880s, for the run to Australia, suggested otherwise:

'*The figures given us with regard to the consumption of alcoholic liquors will no doubt prove a shock to many of our temperance friends...5,000 quarts and 8,000 pints of English beer, 1,000 quarts and 5,000 pints of stout, 1,500 quarts of lager beer, 1,500 bottles of whiskey, 3,800 bottles of various kinds of wines and 10,000 aerated waters.*'
Scarborough Gazette, Britannia, 9th February 1888

'Having a drink or two' seems to have been a constant pleasure for passengers from every era. One merry party from the North of England, on *Mongolia*, for a cruise of the Mediterranean in 1933, recorded a wide variety of reasons for why they had to continually resort to the bar – celebrating the return of a son who had got lost wandering around the ship, congratulating one of their number who had recovered from sea-sickness, dealing with the frustration of not finding a fourth for cards, it being too hot to dance, and more in a similar ilk. Little wonder then that the dockers at Tilbury would be amazed at the number of empties brought ashore at the end of each run.

> '*Champagne flowed like water on Thursdays and Sundays at dinner. On these occasions I took especial care as to whom I danced with, for half the young fellows were much the worse for it.*'
>
> HARRIET EARLE, 1845

Dancing remained a constant feature of entertainment on board; only the fashions, dances and music changed in the ensuing years. Opposite: Detail from a poster by Fritz Bühler for the Orient Line, 1950s. Above: Dancing on deck. Detail from a P&O postcard c.1905.

Entertainment cards were overprinted on board ship with a full programme
of activities for anyone with a competitive spirit. (Berkeley Sutcliffe, 1953)

ENTERTAINMENT

On the early P&O vessels, on-board activities were somewhat limited by the lack of space particularly on the open decks. Nevertheless, passengers managed to find ways of killing time, as a young man travelling on *Himalaya* recounted to his father in 1854:

'During the day we walk about, read or write and at night we spin yarns, play chess or draughts and a few play cards.... For an hour, morning and evening we have a band, a brass one in the former, and a stringed one in the latter part of the day, in fact the time passes swiftly and very pleasantly.'
William Adamson, *Himalaya*, 23rd January 1854

Passengers naturally gravitated into informal groups to play cards or have a sing-song or even paint:

'Some of our party would thus pass the early part of the day after breakfast, in drawing and water colouring; others would be reading, or studying the maps and tracing the way we were pursuing.'
Captain Albert Hervey, *Hindostan*, 1846

Clubs would form for spurious purposes such as the 'port-wine club': *'meeting every night to discuss matters of importance and port-wine negus!'*

As ships grew in size to accommodate more passengers, with increasingly generous public spaces, entertainment became ever more organised. Again it was the passengers themselves who took the lead, establishing committees, electing chairmen and creating complex, highly political organisations which was entertainment in itself and worthy of note in the on-board newspaper:

'A few hours after leaving [port] *notices were posted in the companion calling a meeting at eight o'clock in the Second Saloon. Attendance was good and Mr J. Longmore was unanimously voted to the Chair. He explained that the meeting had been called for the purpose of organizing a committee for the successful carrying on of concerts, sports etc., and a chairman, general secretary, hon. treasurer, editor of the journal, manager inside games and a committee of three for outdoor sports, and a musical director were appointed.'*
Himalaya Observer, *Himalaya*, 1896

Appointments when they came were not always welcome:

No music room was complete without a piano and a supply of amateur talent (top).
Letter writing, board games and cards in the saloon. (Bottom) (W. W. Lloyd, 1892)

'Repeatedly, through the leisurely course of everyday and night, an orchestra – sweating politely under the punkah-louvres – would take up its station in the palm-tree lounge, playing music to suit the moment. The grand climax in the small hours was a whirling series of old-fashioned waltzes, a gallop, and finally, light dimmed…that last exercise for flagging violins, 'Good Night Sweetheart'…. Then the crowd would brace itself into immobility as the loyal strains of 'God Save the King' floated out through the open windows across the moonlight decks and away into the tropical night.'

HOMEWARD BOUND PASSENGER, *VICEROY OF INDIA*, C.1930S

In the earliest days stewards doubled up as musicians and additional music was provided by passengers. In time, cruising and 'short' voyages on board influenced the introduction of professional musicians and entertainers.

'An awful thing happened to me last night. There was a meeting of the passengers to discuss the organisation of the deck sports, and other entertainments and they chose me as one of the committee. This means that I shall have a lot of work to do and shall have to get to know all the passengers, which is awful....'
Walter Biheller, *China*, 14th October 1927

Although the stewards generally played a little music every day, the majority of concerts and other entertainments were provided by the 'talent' found among the travellers themselves. Many 'a merry song and dance' might, as on board *Oriental* in 1846, last into the morning, closing with a 'merry polka'. If the weather was particularly hot in the Red Sea the Captain's permission would be sought for the piano to be taken on deck and awnings arranged for a makeshift stage. Concerts were particularly popular: *'the ladies demand another concert soon – we shall see – but they are evidently serious and will not be put off.'* A typical programme, on board *Himalaya* in 1896, included a violin selection from *Martha*, a piano selection, a recitation of *In the Engine Shed* and four little maids singing *I Don't Want To Play In Your Yard*.

A special concert or ball was usually organised for the final evening of any voyage. Miss Holmes travelling with her brother, Lord Elgin, to his new appointment as Viceroy of India in 1888, reviewed the mixed offerings of their final evening concert on board *Rome*, which included: two violin solos by Lady Mackenzie, *'some songs sung exquisitely by the clergyman from the Second Saloon'*, a most lugubrious and ridiculous song by a Captain Scheider, which had the audience *'choked with suppressed laughter'*, and an amusing, impromptu song by Captain M, who for his finale leapt *'through the nearest window amidst a storm of applause'*.

Dancing often rounded off the evening's entertainment although some nights were more memorable than others:

'The dance on the 25th was a brilliant success, the ship behaved admirably, only rolling sufficiently now and then to pitch dreamily girating couples into the ventilators...The one-step and the two-step were much appreciated. The Lancers also caused great fun... "Auld Lang Syne" and "God Save the King" terminated a very enjoyable evening; then followed "fall in and follow me" around the deck.'
Marmora Gazette, February 1912

Above: Concerts were generally an amateur affair organised by the appropriate elected committee and held in the music room or on deck. (Detail from a P&O postcard c. 1905)

The Clyde

SOLO 4/-
DUET 4/-
ORCHESTRA 2/-
SEPTETT 1/-

HANHART LITH.

LONDON; CHAPPELL & C.º 50 NEW BOND S.ᵗ CITY BRANCH 14 & 15 POULTRY.

In 1892 the Italian composer Procida Bucalossi composed the P & O
Polka, *dedicating the work to the Directors of the Company.*

'Dress well at meals on any P and O boat. If your vessel is one of the yachting cruises it would be advisable to be prepared for dances, theatricals, concerts and all such like emergencies. In other words take as many dresses and fancy dresses as the yacht allows.'

LADY LISBETH, 16TH FEBRUARY 1895

Fancy dress dilemmas. (Original pen and ink sketch by W.W. Lloyd, 1892)

The 'Fancy Dress Ball' was always a particularly popular event, so much so that some would bring their costumes on board with their luggage. Some outfits were more suitable than others as a young man cautioned his fiancée, soon to follow him out east:

'I want to ask you not to come dressed as a man. Several girls did so last night and several men came dressed as women, but it is not considered in good taste and there were some nasty remarks made behind their backs.'
Walter Biheller, *China*, 19th October 1927

The art of improvisation provided the most fun, putting together outfits from odds and ends found on board or, occasionally, bought from shops at ports of call. Sometimes there would be separate prizes for the best costumes 'brought' on board and the best 'wrought' on board: *'The second prize for men was won by a sheik and for women by a girl who came as Neptune in a wonderful get up composed of boiled lobsters and seaweed.'*

The most common fancy dress characters chosen appear to have been Bedouins, girls in national costumes, monks, scarecrows and, of course, pirates and sailors. As Harry Furniss noted the ladies often sought additional help in their preparations at the Barber's shop:

'Ladies dressing for Fancy balls, which are very popular on board, seek the assistance of the talented artist in hair who combined the office of perruquier with the more commonplace duties demanded by his attentions to his male clients.'
Harry Furniss, 1898

In time professional musicians came to replace the amateurs but not completely until after the Second World War. And the arrival of cinemas on board was the final curtain for passengers' own sketches and playlets.

As the open deck space became larger, the inventive imagination of the sports committee came into action, dreaming up a multitude of permutations and combinations of anything that could be thrown or hit or raced, all in the name of entertainment.

'Today the sheets for the deck games competitions have been put up on the notice board. I have entered for all of them and I hope you do too, my darling. It is the best way to make sure of getting exercise, and also you will get to know the other passengers and enter into the life of the ship.'
Walter Biheller, *China*, 15th October 1927

Above: Fancy dress balls were a universal hit with passengers (Moldavia, *1933*). *Below: For crew 'Crossing the Line' (the Equator) for the first time, provided an opportunity to follow age-old traditions of the Court of King Neptune and Queen Amphitrite.* (Mongolia, *1920s*).

Vignettes of deck life on Viceroy of India *(Michel, 1939)*

Little rings of rope or quoits were the most common things to be thrown. A variety of games used them, from deck quoits (where they were thrown towards a concentric target marked on the deck with chalk, with different numbers for the circles reached); deck tennis (where the quoit had to be caught and immediately returned in the hope that your opponent missed it or dropped it); and bucket quoits (where the quoits had to be thrown into buckets some 30 feet away).

In 'bluff,' little canvas bags of sand were thrown at a board divided into twelve squares, ten numbered, and the two top corners with letters 'B' in them. The board was raised at one end and one scored by getting into the numbered squares in order.

Imaginations were fertile when it came to races (often with men and women partnered together), from the writing of telegrams, the lighting of cigarettes and the threading of needles, to the more common egg-and-spoon and potato races. And then there were the 'animal' races – wooden dogs, frogs or horses were attached by strings to poles or handles, generally operated by ladies, with the men betting on likely winners.

Teams were concocted in a variety of ways; first versus second class, passengers versus crew, passengers versus port teams, and so on. Ladies teams were always an attraction as observed by a male passenger in 1896:

'A ladies' cricket match on board is great fun, although the balls thrown overboard in their flight ostensibly towards the wickets made it somewhat expensive for the Quartermaster who manufactures them.'
Fred Reynolds, *India*, 1896

However absurd the activity, games did more than relieve the boredom, they provided an opportunity for differences of class and cloth to be forgotten, at least for a time: *'It is a healthy sight to see... a Bishop tuck up his apron over his arm to take part in a 'tug of war' or a society belle do her utmost to win the prize in an "egg and spoon race".'*

By the 1920s and 1930s 'health and beauty' had become fashionable – serious sunbathing, swimming and jogging round the deck joined quoits, tug-of-war and ping pong in the list of popular pursuits. At the same time purpose-built swimming pools came to replace the makeshift canvas constructions put up on deck, with their allotted times for bathing for men, mixed groups and crew.

When not actually playing a game, P&O passengers could always be relied on to be betting on one, or indeed anything else:

Opposite: New ships of the 1920s and 1930s incorporated permanent pools replacing the makeshift canvas arrangements of earlier years. (Detail from an Orient line poster, 1930s)

Deck games: tug of war (above) and races (below) on Viceroy of India in the 1930s; deck cricket on Strathmore (opposite top) and deck tennis on Moldavia in 1935 (opposite bottom).

'…we had some excellent athletic sports. Tugs of war for the ladies and gentlemen, cockfights, donkey races, in this race the jockey having to drink a glass of water with a teaspoon, the donkey to eat a dry ship's biscuit, both being fed by one of the ladies, the winner having to show his mouth perfectly clear — very awkward for the donkey.'

EDWARD RAWDIN, *VECTIS*, 1905

'The spirit of gambling rules the roost on most ocean liners; every possible contingency is made the subject of bets and sweeps. What time we shall tie up at the next port; whether the pilot will first put his right or left foot aboard, but the never-failing subject is the number of knots in the daily run of the steamer.'
Fred Reynolds, *India*, 1896

Well into the inter-war years betting on the run remained part of the daily schedule under the watchful eye of the Sweepstake Committee. A souvenir log of a voyage from London to Sydney recorded:

'Sweepstakes at 6d per entry were held daily, Sundays excepted, during the voyage and prizes distributed as early as possible after the distance run to 12 noon was published by the ship's authorities. Prizes were allotted on the following proportion of the total daily receipts: — 1st Prize 50 per cent; 2nd Prize 25 per cent…Seamen's Charities, 10 per cent.'
W. North White, *Bendigo*, 1924

Sundays were the exception, betting being supplanted by the act of worship. The august duty fell to the Captain to conduct the Sunday service and pray for the safety of those aboard, for peace, for the moral welfare of the single young men going out to seek their fortunes, and for the health of the Royal family of the day:

'…at seven bells, suddenly a bell began to toll very much like that of a country church, and on going on deck we found an awning raised, a desk with a flag flung over it close to the compass, and the ship's company and passengers assembled there to hear the Captain read the Service in a manly respectful voice.'
William Makepeace Thackeray, 1846

Another account of a service in 1886 suggests that such gatherings engendered 'high thoughts' in their reverential participants:

'There are few religious functions, I think, more impressive than a service on the open waters in the saloon…the table draped with the Union Jack; the hymnals all 'coiled down' against the moment when the harmonium shall resound…the Captain himself, gallant and solemn…the long rows of beautiful or gentle and highbred feminine faces, of brave and dutiful English gentlemen bound on

Opposite: 'Putting up the run' – the daily log was viewed with the utmost interest among the betting fraternity on board and dutiful diary writers. P&O Sketches in Pen & Ink, *Harry Furniss, 1898.*

Above: With the Captain, or a man of the cloth, and a Union Jack on the makeshift pulpit, the dining saloon was quickly converted into a place of worship.

'It is always considered by the passengers a great privilege to be allowed to visit the engine rooms, and parties of ladies, under the escort of one of the gallant ship's officers, may frequently be seen admiring the brightly polished brasswork, and the huge cylinders and levers with their rhythmical motion.'

HARRY FURNISS, 1898

After the steep descent into the ship's bowels the engine room of Himalaya *(built in 1892) was an impressive sight.*

the service of the Queen or the honourable toils of business abroad — all these assembled upon the bosom of the great deep for worship.'
Edwin Arnold, *Parramatta*, 1886

Any man of the cloth was allowed to hold a service on Sunday evening, having first obtained the Captain's permission. Often this led to some rather irreligious, competitive behaviour or, at worst, open warfare between the different sects from High Church to rabid non-conformism.

Besides the pleasure of the ever-changing scenery, the ship itself was a constant source of interest, and organised parties were scheduled for 'visits of inspection'. Each group was accompanied by an officer, who provided information and answered questions. Refrigeration was a matter of much curiosity when it came aboard the 'Jubilee' ships in the 1880s:

'It is worth while paying a visit to the refrigerating chambers, especially if the day is sultry. The visitor who penetrates to these frozen recesses steps at once, by the process of passing through the door, from the atmosphere of a Sydney summer afternoon into a region of frost and snow, where the thermometer registers anything between freezing point and zero.'
Scarborough *Gazette*, *Britannia*, 9th February 1888

Bridge visits were particularly popular:

'The other evening the navigation bridge was opened for inspection for an hour so I went up with a crowd of others & found it most interesting. I asked the sailor at the wheel to take his hands off for a while just to see what would happen, if anything, & was interested to see how the ship immediately changed course and veered to port side.'
Edith Starling, *Rawalpindi*, 1938

And for a lucky few there was a tour of the galleys:

'Next day we toured the ship's kitchens, a fascinating sight to any housewife. Enormous hot plates down the centre flanked by small rooms each with its Goanese workers, each for a special purpose — salads, fish, bread, pastries etc. We came away impressed by the organisation.'
Mrs M. A. Watts, *Arcadia*, 16th March 1963

From Sunday service to quoits, passengers could take or leave the entertainments on offer. But one tradition of shipboard life was compulsory — the muster or safety drill — considered by some an irksome bore, by others, from the following strictures, a waste of time but necessary all the same:

'They have a drill almost as soon as you get on board and all passengers are asked to put on their life belts when the danger bell rings, and assemble on the top deck. Lots of passengers, especially the young girls, often say "oh nonsense, lets escape it and stay in our cabins, it looks too silly to walk about with a life belt on". But I say…discipline. So every time they have life boat drill, sweetheart, don't shirk it.'
Walter Biheller, *China* 14th October 1927

When not fully occupied on board there were often opportunities for going ashore when the ship was in port. This could be just for a few hours, or, when major coaling was taking place, or mail or freight brought aboard, it could be for a day, or more, sometimes involving overnight stays in hotels or hostelries if schedules permitted.

'It was hinted to us that we had better not remain on board whilst the ship was "coaling", as all the cabins and saloons would be shut up to prevent the coal dust from penetrating into them; and any body staying during the process, would be covered with filth, if not suffocated; so we made up our little parcels in our carpet bags and the whole posse of passengers went on shore, amounting to between seventy and eighty in number, presenting a goodly array, and affording excellent opportunities for the hotel and inn-keepers to make a little money.'
Captain Albert Hervey, *Hindostan*, 1846

Early passengers could organise their own trips ashore, taking whatever local transport was available. Later, with the growth in touring and cruising, commercially organised excursions or 'expeditions' were offered by travel agencies or P&O. A couple travelling on *Vectis* used the services of Thomas Cook:

'The next morning we left the ship at eight o'clock, having placed ourselves entirely in the hands of Messrs. Thomas Cook & Son, whose able organiser, Mr. Dosse, is second to none and we are very grateful for all his kindness to us during our many journeys.'
Edward Rawdin, *Vectis*, 1905

Aside from short trips ashore, Thomas Cook was able to offer complete tours of India where it established offices in Bombay, Calcutta and Delhi. Cook's passage to India was via P&O steamers and by an agreement made in 1888 the Company received a sliding scale of commissions for such bookings. When wireless telegraphy came into use a special code denoted the P&O berths so booked – 'Addict' for gentlemen and 'Adder' for ladies.

'We slowly steamed into Port Said about 2.30… What a scene I found myself in on landing! Just thro' the custom's sheds, where Cooks' men, Frenchmen & Arab were shouting at each other, into the streets, green trees on either side, and the most delightful of Eastern shops! But I could not feel it was real. I felt as if I was at an Egyptian Exhibition at Earls Court….'

LENA BIGSBY, *MACEDONIA*, C.1910

Brochures painted a romantic picture of the exoticism of the East. (Greig, 1934)

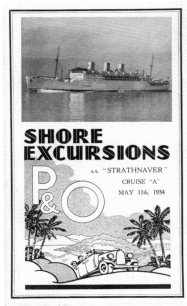

Tales of trips ashore and sight-seeing occupied many a lengthy letter and diary written on board. And then there was the souvenir shopping:

'Next morning we spent in the bazaars, buying many things, which we had sent to England, and before we had finished Mr. Kingsford had spent more than sixty pounds. Amongst the things sent were some lovely carpets, ladies' shawls etc…On Monday an exhibition was held of the goods brought by each passenger during their tour….'
Edward Rawdin, *Vectis*, 1905

Half a century later Mrs Watts succumbed to the temptation of precious stones in Ceylon and shoes in Hong Kong:

'It is extraordinary doing business here…each stone you asked for was offered from countless tissue paper wrappings, all in shoe boxes. I was terribly tempted. There were boxes of topaz, rubies, sapphires, but I was guarded against further extravagance by my pocket.'

'Of course made to measure crocodile shoes and handbags can be produced overnight. They come aboard, place a piece of paper on the deck and draw round your feet, this is all they need and the shoes are brought to the ship the following day.'
Mrs M. A. Watts, *Arcadia*, 21st March 1963

But perhaps the main and most enduring interest of all who had once travelled on P&O ships was their fellow passengers:

'The observer of charades has much to interest and amuse him in studying the idiosyncrasies of his fellow voyagers, for in the comparatively small compass of the ship's saloon you will probably rub shoulders with a greater variety of men and women than in most gatherings of a similar number of people.'
George Henderson, *Rome*, 16th March 1901

Diaries and letters home, over the years, were filled with countless descriptions of those with whom they shared their voyage.

Packed in trunks waiting to be rediscovered were — and are — souvenir programmes, logs and menu cards covered with autographs and personal messages; the tangible reminders of how they had become so intimate, so indecently quickly, with perfect strangers, taking them to their bosoms and swearing eternal friendships:

'Many friendships and intimacies are found on board which may last through life, and a P&O quarter deck… is responsible for many gallant, or learned or commonplace young men, and beautiful or accomplished or clever young women "finding their fate"…happy marriages have resulted from a casual acquaintance found under "the flag that's waved for sixty years in all the Eastern Seas.".'
George Henderson, *Rome*, 16th March 1901

A selection of shore excursion brochures (above) and photographs from albums in the P&O Collection dating from 1930s (opposite)

Cook's Staff

'No one on board can quite relax

Poor Mr Frith gets drunk

And Mrs Frobisher, bathed in tears,

Sits, surrounded by souvenirs

Each one of which she carefully packs

With her hopes, in her cabin trunk…

Last-minute packing finished and done

The long and wearisome journey over

The Governor's Lady, standing apart,

With a sudden lifting of her heart

Sees, like sentinels in the sun,

The arrogant cliffs of Dover.'

NOËL COWARD, *P. & O. 1930*

*Opposite: Four year old Anthony Ashbolt and First
Officer Roy Cookman the familiar faces of the
award winning 'Run Away to Sea' posters of 1958.
Right: Wood engraving on Japanese paper from a
series by Robert Gibbings for the Orient Line. (1932)*

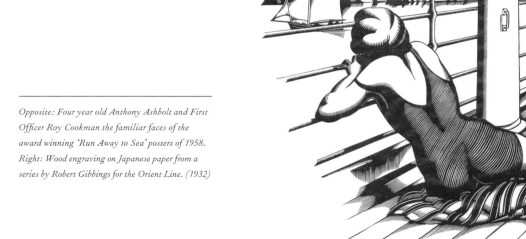

'The P&O Heritage Collection, with its vast and diverse collections from archives to art, furniture to films, menus to murals, photographs to plates and almost everything in between, tells the unique story of P&O and nearly two centuries of British shipping along the way.'

nlike many company collections, P&O's was not the private passion of one Chairman, nor the latest investment idea of another, nor could it be accused of being 'art for art's sake'. Most of what was 'collected' was done so in the daily course of business; ship models with ship contracts, portraits for posterity and posters for promotion. But what assured their preservation was the pomp of and pride in P&O, which began in the earliest days and still prevails today.

'[P&O] has now attained to a magnitude and national importance unprecedented in the annals of private maritime enterprise in this or any country of the world – a circumstance which I cannot help regarding with strong feelings of pride'
Arthur Anderson, 12th June 1854

EARLY PURCHASES

The founders of P&O were convinced of their part in making history. Theirs was not simply a steamer service, it was a 'great national undertaking' and, as befits such historic endeavours, each pioneering step was charted, celebrated and often painted.

The first pictures to adorn the walls of the Peninsular Steam Navigation Company offices (at St Mary Axe)

The Company's ship models and paintings, on display in 1891 in the P&O pavilion at the Royal Naval Exhibition, London.

were painted by a local artist, Stephen Dadd Skillett, in the formative years of the Company's foundation. The Peninsular ships *Braganza* and *Royal Tar* were depicted steaming through calm, or rough, waters with the Iberian mails. Although owned by Captain Richard Bourne, the ships were painted flying the pennant of the new Peninsular Company. The flag combined the colours of the Royal houses of Spain and Portugal – red and yellow for the Bourbons, blue and white for Braganza – as bold in Skillett's day as they remain today.

In 1843, the P&O Board acquired a painting by the established marine artist William John Huggins, commemorating the historic departure of *Hindostan* from Southampton to open the Indian mail service. Like many other additions to the collection, it started with a speculative approach by the artist:

'Read a letter from Mr Huggins Marine Painter dated 24th inst offering 40 proofs of the Hindostan *with the original painting for 40 guineas which was agreed to'.*
P&O Board Minutes, 25th July 1843

Artistic attention turned next to the men behind the ships. The sudden death of one of the three Managing Directors, Francis Carleton, at just forty-eight, couldn't fail to remind those around him of their own impermanence.

*Above: Portraits of P&O's founding fathers graced the boardroom walls of the
Company's offices at Leadenhall Street, both old and new. (New boardroom, c. 1970)*

Portraits were painted of Willcox, Anderson and Bourne, who now made up the triumvirate of founding fathers, together with James Allan, Carleton's replacement, and Sir John Pirie, then Chairman. The artist chosen was Thomas Francis Dicksee who, typically for the time, painted his subjects life-size. The portraits were a gift to the Board by Sir John Pirie in 1850. It was a timely gesture – within a year both Bourne and Pirie himself had died.

Beyond mere decoration, paintings and models had a purpose. They were used at the Company's offices to show a merchant or passenger the ship in which their precious cargo, or they, might sail. To illustrate the voyage itself, and the route taken to India, there was an altogether more immersive and entertaining experience in the form of a moving exhibition or 'diorama'.

The diorama entitled *Overland Route of the Mail from Southampton to Calcutta* was produced by the artists Thomas Grieve and William Telbin, with the help of P&O. In addition to a financial contribution, the Company granted the artists free passage to Spain and Portugal 'for the purpose of taking sketches' and lent oriental costumes for the performance, which opened in 1850, at the elegant 'Gallery of Illustration' in London's Regent Street. The diorama consisted of over thirty full-size, painted scenes on a revolving stage, accompanied by a learned commentary and 'a musical descriptive fantasia' inspired by the ports and places en route: a *Fandango* for Tarifa, *Rule Britannia* and *The Spanish Contrabandist* for Gibraltar, a *Moorish March* for Algiers, an *Arabian Hymn* for Jeddah, and finally the 'National Anthem' on reaching Calcutta. The diorama was a great success attracting audiences of over 200,000 in the first year, and much critical acclaim:

'*Each tableau is so perfect that it fixes itself indelibly in the memory. The first glance at the exquisite views of Malta, for instance, floods the mind of the spectator, and imparts a notion of climate which the finest oral description would fail to give.*'
The Morning Chronicle, 22nd October 1850

The long list of distinguished visitors included Prince Albert, who attended with several of his children. The diorama was recreated in an album of watercolours, presented to Brodie McGhie Willcox, and engraved as plates in the book of *The Route of the Overland Mail to India* which followed.

Above: Braganza *painted in 1837, one of five works by Stephen Dadd Skillett in the P&O Heritage Collection.*

Overleaf: A moving diorama opened in 1850 and told the story of the passage of mail from Southampton to Calcutta by P&O steamer and 'overland' from Alexandria to Suez.

GENEROUS GIFTS

P&O did much to improve the Overland Route and support the development of Egypt's infrastructure and the Company's contribution did not go unnoticed. In 1865, Pasha Ismail, Egypt's ruler, hosted a public reception for the P&O Board at the Citadel in Cairo and presented the Company with one of the most significant gifts in the collection. This impressive *garniture de cheminée*, consisting of a stunning silver clock and two vases, elaborately decorated with sphinxes and ancient hieroglyphics, was a tangible reminder of the 'special' relationship that existed between country and Company.

In 1854 P&O profits plummeted. For the first time there was no dividend for shareholders, and Anderson was forced to acknowledge at the half-yearly meeting:

'I am afraid that some of you, after hearing our Half-Yearly Report, may go away under the impression that the "rising sun" of the "Peninsular and Oriental Company" is about to become a setting one – and may, perhaps, rush into the market to sell your Shares. Now, I believe no such thing. Although our sun may appear, just now, partially obscured, believe me it is only a passing cloud, and that it will, before long, shine out with its accustomed brilliancy (Cheers)'
Arthur Anderson, 12th June 1854

In a show of solidarity, Willcox and Anderson announced that they were relinquishing forthwith a percentage of their commission to set up a 'Provident and Good Service Fund', to reward and encourage 'talent' within the Company and provide welfare for P&O employees.

It was a generous gesture and a stroke of genius in investor relations, whether by intent or not. Distracted from their loss of dividend, the shareholders busily preoccupied themselves with procuring fitting 'testimonials of valuable and lasting character' to present to both men. Two silver dinner services were commissioned from the London silversmiths, Smith Nicholson & Sons, each to the value of £1,500. They were identical, save for the addition of the family crests of Willcox and Anderson, and featured a spectacular centrepiece, four feet in height and weighing over 770 ounces. In time the services became heirlooms, Willcox specifying in his will that the centrepiece be held by his son for life before passing to the eldest son of his daughter. Anderson, having no heirs, bequeathed his service to the 'Directors of P&O' with the sum of £1,000 for the purpose of forming a fund 'for an

A striking silver 'garniture de cheminée' was presented to the Company by Pasha Ismail, the ruler of Egypt in 1865.

annual dinner in commemoration of the establishment of the said company'. For many years since, the 'Anderson Silver' has graced the table of many a management dinner and significant occasion in the Company's history.

PAINTINGS, PAVILIONS & PENCILLINGS

P&O survived the low of 1854, the crisis of 1867 and the challenges of post-Suez years, to reach the age of fifty. The year was 1887 and it was also the Golden Jubilee year of Queen Victoria's reign. P&O's Jubilee provided the Company with an opportunity to celebrate, with pride, their progress so far. A set of composite paintings were commissioned from the artist R. H. Neville-Cumming which trumpeted not only the new 'Jubilee' class ships, but significant achievements in the fleet's progression from the 206-ton paddle steamer *William Fawcett* to the 5,000-ton *Carthage*, fitted with searchlights to be the first steamer to transit the Suez Canal at night in 1886.

The 'Jubilee' paintings were a feature of P&O's impressive pavilion for the Royal Naval Exhibition in 1891. Described as one of the 'prettiest and most interesting' pavilions in the exhibition, it was built to the design of Thomas Edward Collcutt. Inside there were 'courteous attendants' to tell you all about the 'history and operations of this great company'. The interior was adorned with P&O's collection of paintings and models of ships, past and present, and specially commissioned panels by Frank Murray painted in oils on an unusual gold and silver ground. The panels, eight in total, took as their theme famous epochs in the history of shipping and the four corners of the compass. In 1893 the panels were installed permanently in the boardroom of Collcutt's new building for the Company in Leadenhall Street.

Some years earlier Collcutt had also designed Sutherland's country estate, Coldharbour. As the Chairman's daughter recounted, Sutherland considered the house his creation; in furnishing and decoration 'his was the ruling taste'. Described

Two identical, solid silver nine-light centrepieces (4ft in height) were presented to Arthur Anderson and Brodie McGhie Willcox by P&O's shareholders in 1855.

Above: Queen Victoria visiting the P&O pavilion at the Royal Naval Exhibition in 1891. The pavilion was later sold, dismantled and re-erected in Devonshire Park, Eastbourne.

as a collector, in a light-hearted fashion, Sutherland moved in artistic circles and was a good friend and client of the painter James McNeill Whistler. When the time came for Sutherland himself to be painted, it may have been Whistler who recommended his fellow American and former pupil, John Singer Sargent, then enjoying considerable success as a society portrait painter in London. Before taking its place in the P&O boardroom, Sargent's portrait was exhibited at the Royal Academy in London in 1898 where it attracted the attention of the *Punch* satirists, who published their own version entitled *Peninsular & Oriental, Pines, Prunes and Prisms* in a reference to Dickens. Elsewhere in the Press the portrait was well received and still today lives up to the compliment paid to it more than a century ago:

'With as few strokes of the brush as may be he [Sargent] *places the sitter before us as a living man on the canvas.'*
Morning Post, 12th May 1898

Under Sutherland P&O embraced the opportunities afforded by improved printing techniques to publicise both the Company and the experience of travelling by sea. The first *P&O Pocket Book* was published in 1888. Intended as a useful companion en route, it gave readers the Chairman's own account of P&O's history, as well as descriptions of ports and places, tips for travellers at sea and agents' details. After 10,000 copies were issued, a second edition (with maps) followed in 1890. *P&O Pencillings* by William Whitelock Lloyd appeared in 1892, full of colour illustrations and witty observations of life on board a P&O steamer. Lloyd was already known to the Company as an artist and he travelled to and from India in *Britannia*, *Arcadia* and *Mirzapore*. 'Pencillings' became a firm favourite and the colour plates were made into a set of lantern slides.

Harry Furniss was best known for his illustrations for both Dickens and Thackeray, and his acerbic, political sketches in *Punch*, where he was employed for many years. Although Furniss found plenty of amusement on his P&O passage to Australia, he was rather less satirical than usual with the characters he encountered. In 1898 he exhibited a hundred drawings of his voyage at the Fine Art Society in London and published *P&O Sketches in Pen & Ink* in the same year.

Opposite and above top: Elaborate panels, painted by Frank Murray, were displayed at the Royal Naval Exhibition in 1891 and 1892, before finding a permanent home in the boardroom of a new extension to Leadenhall Street completed in 1893.

A 1908 brochure for Vectis *illustrated by Charles Dixon.*

ART FOR ADVERTISING SAKE

*'For heaven's sake let us abandon the old cliché that art plays
no part in advertising.'*
Norman Wilkinson, 1969

With the introduction of cruising in 1904 the whole business
of P&O's advertising was to change. The Company had to
attract new passengers drawn to P&O not by 'need' but by
'want'. For the new leisure traveller, it was the spaciousness of
the accommodation, or the exoticism of the tour destinations,
that now determined the line of choice. A whole new publicity
department was set up to design, produce and distribute
advertisements and brochures to the Company's growing
number of agents and interested passengers:

*'So runs the P&O advertisement; those who wish to know more
of this alluring holiday scheme will obey the behest of the three
concluding words and "write for programme." '*
P&O Brochure, 1910

The first brochures included deck plans and black-and-
white interior photographs for the cruising yacht *Vectis*.
Within a year or two the brochures, or 'artistic booklets'
as they became known, were increasingly colourful, often
illustrated by well-known maritime artists like Charles
Dixon RI and William Lionel Wyllie RA. Wyllie travelled
in *Vectis* to Norway producing a series of paintings which
he exhibited in 1907, to less than critical acclaim:

*'These records, at the Fine Art Society's rooms, of P and O cruises
"from Spitsbergen to the Golden Horn" show Mr Wyllie with all
his accomplishments, but also with the want of high cultivation on
the side of colour that tends in an increased degree to modify our
admiration of his work...he who once was a colourist may produce
very poor colour indeed.'*
Athenaeum, 9th March 1907

The high colour translated well into print and the scenes
found a more natural, if commercial, home in P&O's brochures
and Wyllie's own book *'Norway and its Fjords'* published in 1909.

In spite of their more mercantile pursuits, both Wyllie
and Dixon continued to exhibit regularly at the traditional
institutions of the Royal Academy and Royal Institution, where
their reputations were founded. And P&O acquired many of
their original works, in both oils and watercolours, establishing
a sizeable collection of works by Charles Dixon in particular.

Top: The 1907 brochure for Vectis *featured watercolours by W. L. Wyllie. Bottom:
Known as 'artistic booklets', early brochure covers for cruising were particularly decorative.*

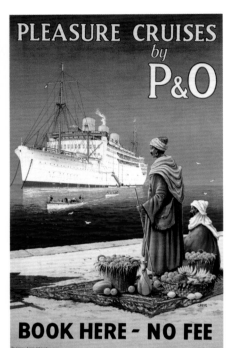

Postcards and posters were a natural progression of the growth in chromo lithography. The printers, Andrew Reid & Co., led the way creating colour postcards for P&O and the earliest poster surviving in the collection, produced for the Orient Line in 1895. Like so many early posters the artist was chosen by the printer and was one of his own staff artists. For many years, and in many companies, printers controlled the choice of artist presenting speculative *faits accomplis* to those in the market for a poster:

'Word had got round like wildfire that the firm was out for a shipping poster and a number of printing firms had promptly commissioned artists to make designs on the chance of getting an order'.
Norman Wilkinson, 1969

The artist Norman Wilkinson PPRI was keen to elevate the art of poster beyond what he termed the 'commodity posters' or the printers' creations. He forged his own revolution in railway posters with an exhibition of Royal Academicians' Posters in 1924, which had a profound effect on poster design far beyond the tracks.

The traditional style for shipping posters placed the ship centre stage exaggerating, where possible, both its mass and its might. Early P&O line voyage posters by Frank Mason RI and H. K. Rooke RA conformed to type but with the growth in cruising, designs for posters in the 1930s

focused more on colourful destinations and ports of call, and P&O followed suit.

Although they mirrored the mood, and moved with the times, the Company's posters were seldom revolutionary, unlike some on the railways or those of the Orient Line. Instead they reflected an eclectic choice of artists including some of the Company's own.

In the interwar years, the publicity department and P&O's artists were kept busy producing decorative menus, port information and tour leaflets (which were to be 'overprinted' on board ship) and larger, glossier brochures and colour advertisements. The latter were required to fill the prime, and only colour spot, in the monthly sea travel magazine, *The Blue Peter*, launched in 1921, with P&O as the lead advertiser. The covers of *The Blue Peter* featured the paintings of Jack Spurling, a number of which were acquired to grace P&O's office walls.

PAST & PRESENT

In 1937 P&O turned one hundred and marked the occasion with dinners, celebrations and services both ashore and aboard. As the centenary year coincided with the Coronation of King George VI, P&O decorated the facade of the Passenger Office in Cockspur Street, which was on the

---

*Above: Traditionally the design of line voyage posters focused on the ship (*Ballarat, *Herbert K Rooke, 1911), but 'the destination' was of more importance for cruise posters (Greig, 1930s).*

Opposite: Baradine *painted by Frank Mason as a design for a poster advertising P&O's Branch Service to Australia via the Cape (c. 1922).*

processional route. Banners boldly asserted the Company's age and size, flying the flag for P&O, BI, NZSCo., Union Steam and the Orient Line, who occupied the western end of the building. A special centenary supplement appeared in *The Times* and P&O commissioned Norman Wilkinson to paint the Company's first paddle steamer *William Fawcett* and latest liner *Stratheden*. Prints were made from the paintings and distributed in huge numbers by the Company.

P&O called on Wilkinson again in darker days. *Rawalpindi*, serving as an armed merchant cruiser, had been an early casualty of the Second World War, with a terrible loss of life. Wilkinson painted the last hours of the ship a year later, in 1940, building up the scene from the facts reported and with the accuracy of one who, as a young Naval reservist, had invented 'dazzle camouflage' in the First World War:

'I was always at pains to reach for the greatest possible accuracy, whilst at the same time allowing myself the freedom to paint worth-while pictures, rather than photographic records.'
Norman Wilkinson, 1969

Wilkinson's work was considered so accurate that P&O had to seek permission from the Admiralty to reproduce the painting for relatives of P&O crew lost on board. Permission was granted but only on condition that the image couldn't be published for the duration of the War.

'Although the ship has gone, this picture shows positions of guns and alterations to the appearance which might indicate what has been done with other converted ships'.
P&O Managing Directors, c. 1940

At the end of the war, P&O staff returned to central London from their secret wartime offices, known only as 'somewhere in the country'. They had been lucky: the Company's offices, with their collections, were intact and ready to be reoccupied. Orient Line had not been so fortunate, its head office in Fenchurch Avenue had been bombed in 1941 with the loss of the company's entire archive.

Perhaps mindful of the fragility of P&O's own historical treasures the Company established its first in-house museum in 1952. Museums, as they were keen to stress, *'are by no means dry-as-dust repositories. How could they be when they hold tangible proofs of the reality of history?'* The museum brought together the Company's

Rawalpindi *under fire from German battle cruisers* Scharnhorst *and* Gneisenau *in the North Atlantic before it sank on 23rd November 1939 with a great loss of life. (Norman Wilkinson). Overleaf: A sailor-made model of* Hindostan *of 1842 sits alongside the Company's third supplemental charter dated 1854.*

existing archives, together with models, artefacts, and art, augmented with donations from former staff and 'generous friends overseas'. Whilst the museum may not have been as unique as the new P&O house magazine, *About Ourselves*, proudly proclaimed, it certainly was: *'a collection of shipping items unrivalled in the City of London'* at the time.

The first major addition to the museum, in 1952, was P&O's first, and only, foray into art as an investment. A collection of watercolours by the celebrated eighteenth-century artists, William and Thomas Daniell, was offered for private sale. Unlike everything else in the Company's possession, the collection bore no direct relevance to P&O, nor any of its shipping lines. But the watercolours were all views of India and, in that respect, they couldn't fail to attract the attention of Sir William Currie. The contact came through the Chairman's good friend, Sir John Burder, who had numerous links with India. In total there were 108 paintings making it the largest single collection of 'Daniells' in existence. Once in P&O's collection the Daniells were exhibited publicly at the Commonwealth Institute in London and later the Smithsonian Institute in Washington. For a further two decades, the collection remained intact before a number of them were sold in 1974. The remainder attracted record prices at auction in 1996. Return on investment had been very good indeed.

MODERN TIMES

The 1950s saw the arrival of a more modern look to the Company and its offices in Cockspur Street. The P&O lettering was restyled by Edward Burrett and adverts now bore the strapline 'A Commonwealth Lifeline' replacing the Empire of old. New neon signage was hoisted on to the facade and a large illuminated revolving globe suspended above the front door. The large traditional shipbuilders' models, with their meticulously detailed gold plated fittings, which had graced the office windows in the 1920s, were eclipsed by smaller lightweight 'travel agents' models, produced in bulk and shipped to the windows of agents all over the world. New window displays were crafted in card, paper and plastic, as elaborate and dramatic as stage sets and equally demountable. Cockspur Street's windows now glowed at night with the creations of Barbara Brook, Zygmunt Kowalewski and C. A. Neville Parker.

At Leadenhall Street there was a facelift for the City passenger office, which opened in 1957 with dynamic

The first Company museum was established at Leadenhall Street in 1952 as a: 'tribute to the men and the ships of past generations'.

'...*the architects brought in many of P&O's oil paintings and old travel posters in an attempt to humanise the working environment.*'

INTERIOR DESIGN, JULY 1972

The new P&O building (on the site of the old) was modern, sophisticated and respectful of the Company's rich heritage.

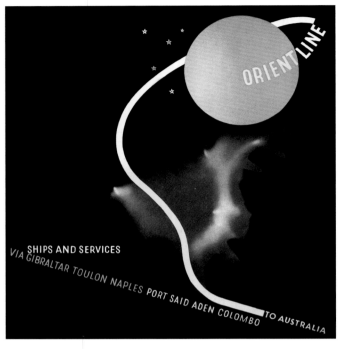

window displays, earning P&O the accolade of 'a real go-ahead firm' and provoking the timely comparison: *'they're taking a leaf out of the airlines book'*. In truth, the real inspiration was much closer to hand. The Orient Line had long perfected the art of window display and collaborated with P&O on a number of occasions. In matters of design, art and advertising, Orient Line remained fashionably 'ahead' of P&O throughout its history.

Window displays and models were the responsibility of the P&O Publicity Department in addition to commissioning photographs, posters and all other printed material. In the 1950s, the department produced eight to twelve posters a year, which were designed to be used in a number of different countries and frequently in conjunction with BI.

'Ideas are born in the department and first take shape as a "rough" sketch for a poster or a "dummy" for a booklet.... Knowing what we want we try to choose the artists best suited to carry out the type of work required.'
About Ourselves, March 1954

Often the artist was one of P&O's own and, just occasionally, their work was recognised in the wider and higher echelons of the design journals like *Modern Publicity*. More often than not the plaudits were reserved for Orient Line's advertising, which relied on the brilliance of a whole host of leading artists from McKnight Kauffer Hon RDI to Graham Sutherland RSA and Abram Games RDI.

In the late 1950s P&O and Orient Line's publicity departments collaborated on a number of joint advertising initiatives to reach new audiences in America. Now more than ever both P&O and Orient needed to attract more passengers to compete with the airlines. Their two latest superliners, *Oriana* and *Canberra*, were widely heralded with all new 'singing and dancing' ship models doing the rounds of the global trade fairs. These futuristic models were interactive, with moving parts and push button lights showing every passenger aspect of the ships.

There was a new 'modernity' about the company and with it came two new head offices growing in tandem at opposite ends of the world in London and Sydney. The London office at Leadenhall Street attracted acclaim in the design press, Michael Manser RA describing it in 1970 as *'one of the most dramatic and sophisticated pieces of commercial building yet seen in London'*. At the core of the successful design was Sir Colin Anderson, a Director of P&O and so long the pioneer of Orient Line's design sophistication.

Top: Orient Line brochure designed by Edward McKnight Kauffer in 1937.
Bottom: One of a handful of posters designed for the Orient Line by Abram Games (1956).

Opposite: P&O House at Cockspur Street with a flag pole in place of the original crowning cupola, which was never replaced after the Second World War. (May 1970).

In a fitting tribute to the enduring nature of his influence a large model of *Orion* built in 1935 graced the Directors' floor where he was to be found. On the Chairman's floor above, a huge 'builder's' model of *Ranpura* from 1925 sat comfortably with a contemporary portrait of Sir Donald Anderson by Derek Hill. In the basement there was a stunning new Company museum designed by Robert Whetmore. The overall effect was one which could equally apply to P&O's Head Office, thirty-five years later:

'A mature, united and homogenous design whose modernism is balanced by the display of historic relics and models acquired over the Company's long trading history.'
Michael Manser, 1970

BEYOND THE OFFICE

With the radical restructuring of the P&O Group, which began in 1971, the art and archive collections of the different shipping lines in the group came together for the first time. The archives, which occupied over 2,000 feet of shelf space, found a new public home in the National Maritime Museum in Greenwich, where they remain on loan today.

The National Maritime Museum had been established in the same year as the Company's centenary and many loans from P&O's collection date back to the Museum's formative years.

For the Company's earliest connections to museums one has to go right back to 1868 and the new South Kensington Museum, which had recently started a collection of ship models and marine engines. P&O lent a model of *Surat* (built just two years before in 1866) and more loans followed, in 1878 and 1907, including a model of the engines of the ill-fated *Carnatic* which was wrecked in 1869. In 1909 the museum took on the more familiar name, the Science Museum, by which we know it today. The P&O models are still on loan to the Science Museum and many loan items can also be seen in regional museums in the United Kingdom and as far afield as Australia and Hong Kong.

Over the years P&O ship models have found welcome homes in nautical training schools and ships including the *Indefatigable* and *HMS Worcester,* so long the cadet ship for P&O Captains and crew. The 'British Ship Adoption Society', which began in the 1930s, encouraged schools to 'adopt a ship' – combining an educational intent with providing moral support for far flung crews. Many a Company officer found himself in the classroom, and bells and models of P&O ships have enjoyed a history all of their own in schools at home and abroad.

Above: Captain Traynier visiting Bolton Girls' School (Tillottson's Newspapers).

Opposite: Cairo painted in the late 1840s: 'No Oriental town more completely realizes the ideas generated by a perusal of the Arabian Nights'. (Henry Fitzcook)

William Ayerst Ingram painted the captivating sight of Britannia *coaling at night in the outer harbour at Aden c.1895.*

ARTISTS & ART AT SEA

Artists have always travelled east and in the early days they went by sea, some by P&O. In the 1840s, Egypt and the Middle East held a particular fascination, perhaps fuelled by a new translation of *The Arabian Nights* by Reverend Edward Lane who lived in Cairo. The artist, David Roberts RA, travelled widely taking a tour in Egypt and the Holy Land in 1838-39 and producing sketches which were later used in the diorama of the Overland Route.

In 1840, Sir David Wilkie sketched the route that Thackeray would later follow, through the Middle East and Egypt. Whilst in Cairo he painted a portrait of the Egyptian ruler (Pasha Muhammad Ali) and in Constantinople the Sultan of Turkey. After a stay at Waghorn's hotel in Alexandria, Wilkie departed for England in P&O's *Oriental*. Close to Gibraltar the artist became gravely ill, watched helplessly by his companion, the P&O surgeon and a second physician who attended him, and died on board on 1st June. As a tribute to the loss of his friend, J. M. W. Turner painted *Peace – Burial at Sea*, exhibiting the work in 1842 with the words:

*'The midnight torch gleamed o'er the steamers side
And merit's corse was yielded to the tide'.*
J. M. W. Turner, 1842

Fortunately there were happier endings to P&O's brushes with artists at sea. The watercolourist, Andrew Nicholl RHA, presented the Board with six paintings of *principal ports visited by the Company's steamers*, in return for free passage granted to his wife, who joined him in Colombo in 1846. Frederick, Lord Leighton PRA was a frequent traveller to the East in P&O steamers between his first visit to Egypt in 1868 and his last to Algiers in 1895 on board *Simla*. Despite his love of travel and the Middle East, Leighton was by his own admission 'a poor sailor at best' and even worse on 'other' ships: *'…three tedious days on board a Russian boat which tossed and rolled like a cork over a sea on which a P&O would have been motionless.'*
Lord Leighton, 18th October 1873

Sir John Lavery travelled to Tangiers where he remained for several months. Returning in 1891, Lavery painted a work known simply as *On board a P. & O.* William Ayerst Ingram created an entire exhibition from his time aboard, entitled *P&O Voyage*, which opened in Glasgow in 1895.

Thanks to his friendship with Sir Thomas Sutherland, Whistler was treated like royalty on his P&O passage:

'Every thing excellent – big boat! – and the Manager on board prowling about to meet the General [Whistler], *and take on personally to Stateroom! Call up Steward and recommend his good conduct and special attention to Sir Thomas' friend!'*
James McNeill Whistler, December 1900

Whistler had been unwell and was prescribed a warmer winter in the Mediterranean. The artist returned some months later having spent the season in Algiers, Marseilles and Corsica. For the maritime painter, William Lionel Wyllie, the main attraction of his travels was the sea itself and the cooler fjords of Norway. In total he spent over three months at sea (between 1906 and 1907) in the company of his wife and Captain A. Thompson, who captained all four of his P&O pleasure cruises. Wyllie painted his watercolours en route, reputedly selling enough to his fellow passengers to pay for his passage.

The presence of art on board dates back to P&O's earliest days, but it was only in later years that individual pictures as opposed to murals featured in decorative schemes. Even in the 1940s there were only a few examples, and some which owed their existence to a happy accident. When the Australian artist, John Loxton, turned up, unannounced, at the P&O offices, as luck would have it, the Company was considering buying some 'Australian' art. Within minutes a deal was done and three of Loxton's landscapes were bought for the Australia room on board *Himalaya*.

It was not until *Canberra* that P&O's first 'on board' collection was acquired and then it was with the close co-operation of the Orient Line. Orient ships had for some time featured collections of emerging and established British and Australian artists such as Edward Bawden RA and Douglas Annand. As well as large murals both produced small framed prints and works which together with prints from respected editions, like the 'School Prints', were used in cabins and, sparingly, in public rooms. The Orient Line approach was adopted for *Canberra* but the choice of artists was 'consciously' different from *Oriana*. For prints, P&O again turned to the Royal College of Art and particularly the works of Edwin La Dell ARA and Alistair Grant. In what had become something of a P&O tradition, *Canberra* was further *'enlivened by paintings depicting various aspects of life 100 years ago.'*

When the time came for *Canberra* to retire from service (unlike too many of its P&O and Orient Line predecessors) the art collection on board was not forgotten. Everything that survived, and could be detached, was painstakingly removed from the ship to join the P&O heritage collections ashore.

Edward Ardizzone, one of Sir Hugh Casson's colleagues at the RCA, was commissioned to paint murals for the First Class Nursery on board Canberra, *including* Treasure Island.

'*P&O! There are other shipping companies with names which can be conveniently reduced to initials, but these are meaningless outside limited circles and the companies concerned frown upon such familiarity. Not so, P&O! For over a century every Britisher with the slightest knowledge of the East has understood what these letters stand for and none but a pedant would dream of giving the name in full.*'

COMMANDER C. R. VERNON GIBBS, 1963

A new P&O neon sign was installed on the front of the Cockspur Street office in 1956, following a new logo typeface designed by Edward Burrett.

'...to the flag lover and historian the perfect flag in some way indicates a history or tradition, a meaning and symbolism of origin – as again heraldic devices usually do. In all these respects the house flag of the P. & O. is one of the most perfect I know.'

BOYD CABLE,1937

SYMBOLS OF PRIDE

Seldom has a company's name or identity prevailed for as long as P&O's. As early as 1844, the Directors were assured of 'our name and influence' and such confidence paid dividends. Although the Company never altered its full legal name, the abbreviation 'P&O' was in colloquial use within the first few years. Indeed the initials were so familiar that they were even adopted as a 'nom de plume' for the author of the novel *Always Ready or Everyone his pride* (by a 'P. & O.') published in 1859.

The initials remained so instantly recognisable that it wasn't until the 1930s that the Company gestured towards a consistent typeface logo. In 1955, Edward Burrett designed a new identity incorporating P&O's 'rising sun' and a decade later this was replaced with a 'shadow' typeface, in a more modern idiom, intended *'to evoke an immediate reaction which if the logo type is successful is a pleasing one'*. Seaman Wilkinson's shadow design continued until 1975, when a comprehensive 'rebrand' by Wolff Olins was launched. The new identity followed the Company's major structural reorganisation, which, in turn, had ended the distinct names and liveries of the individual subsidiary companies. The house flag now became central to the Company's identity and flew once more across the entire fleet and appeared on thousands of vehicles and containers.

The colours of the house flag have remained unchanged

As well as major painting commissions for the Company, Norman Wilkinson produced designs for brochures. (Above: detail of brochure, 1938)

since 1837. The earliest paintings reveal some differences in the shape of the flag (from an early pennant to a rectangle) and which way it was flown, but these anomalies were ironed out by the late 1840s. And lest one forget how to fly the famous flag, there was an easy rhyme to remember: *'Blue to the mast, Red to the fly, Yellow to the deck and White to the Sky'.*

The addition of 'Oriental' to the P&O name in 1840 warranted a new symbol to add to the Company's 'Peninsular' flag. A 'rising sun' motif was adopted and first used on uniforms, swords and crockery before appearing in print in the 1850s. The 'rising sun' was often accompanied by P&O's assumed motto 'Quis Separabit' – who shall divide us – which they shared with the Order of St. Patrick.

From the late 1840s there was a Company badge or crest, which represented P&O mail routes, in the form of a circle quartered and decorated with a figure of Britannia, pyramids (Egypt), an elephant (India), and pagodas (China). In the centre there was a small shield with a paddle steamer surmounted by a 'rising sun'. The form of the badge remained largely unchanged until 1937 when a formal Coat of Arms was applied for. The new centenary Coat of Arms included Australia for the first time (at the expense of Egypt). Only the elephant survived from the earliest days in a design, which now included a Chinese dragon, a British lion and

a kangaroo. The colours of the P&O flag provided the background palette and the 'rising sun' the crest. There was a change too for the company motto, which became 'Quis Nos Separabit' but retained its meaning and sentiment.

From the earliest painting to the latest logo, the importance of the Company's past has always played a part in its present.

'The company has a great past which we can all survey with pride…We shall not pass on to our successors a finer name or higher standard than we inherited.'
About Ourselves, 1956

Pride is never far from P&O. Like an heirloom, and the collection itself, pride has passed from generation to generation throughout the history of the Company. In 1910 Sir Thomas Sutherland ventured to ask for how long the P&O story would continue:

'Well, gentleman, long may this continue. How long? Let us say for another seventy-five years – or, at all events, as much longer as possible.'
Sir Thomas Sutherland, 1910

More than a century later, we're still counting…

CATALOGUE
OF PAINTINGS
ILLUSTRATED

The P&O Heritage Collection
counts amongst its numbers over
500 paintings. The following
catalogue gives brief details for
those illustrated in this book. The
paintings are listed alphabetically
by artist with page references.
Dimensions are 'sight' size and given
in centimetres, height before width.

DOUGLAS ANDERSON
B.1934

Detail from: *Portrait of Kenneth
James William Mackay, third
Earl of Inchcape*, 1983
(three-quarter length, seated)
Oil on board
89.3 x 74.1 cm
P&O Heritage Ref. AC/04185/00
p. 10

EDWARD ARDIZZONE
1900-1971
CBE, RA, RDI

Detail from: *Treasure Island*, c. 1961
Watercolour on melamine-
impregnated paper
241.0 x 457.4 cm
P&O Heritage Ref. AC/01010/02
p. 241

MARCIANO ANTONIO BAPTISTA
1826-1896

*View of the West Part of Victoria, Hong
Kong with the P&O Office*, c. 1852
(assisted by George Chinnery)
Pen and ink and watercolour (with
some bodycolour) on Whatman paper
40.7 x 68.4 cm
P&O Heritage Ref. AC/02130/00
p. 22-23

OSWALD HORNBY JOSEPH BIRLEY
1880-1952
MC, RA

Detail from: *Portrait of The Rt
Hon Alexander Shaw, second
Baron Craigmyle*, 1939
(half length, seated)
Oil on canvas
99.6 x 74.5 cm
P&O Heritage Ref. AC/04184/00
p. 10

GERALD MAURICE BURN
1862-1945

Arcadia at sea, 1889
Oil on canvas
74.5 x 104.8 cm
P&O Heritage Ref. AC/02103/00
p. 26

THOMAS FRANCIS DICKSEE
1819-1895

Detail from: *Portrait of Arthur
Anderson MP*, 1850
(three-quarter length, standing)
Oil on canvas
139.7 x 109.7 cm
P&O Heritage Ref. AC/02132/00
p. 10

Detail from: *Portrait of Brodie
McGhie Willcox MP*, 1850
(three-quarter length, standing)
Oil on canvas
139.7 x 110.5cm
P&O Heritage Ref. AC/02123/00
p. 10

Detail from: *Portrait of Captain
Richard Bourne RN*, 1850
(three-quarter length, standing)
Oil on canvas
139.7 x 109.3 cm
P&O Heritage Ref. AC/02122/00
p. 10

PHILIP DE LASZLO
1869-1937
MVO, PRBA, RP, NPS

Detail from: *Portrait of The
Rt Hon the Earl of Inchcape
GCSI, GCMG, KCIE*, 1921
(three-quarter length, standing)
Oil on canvas
173.99 x 116.8 cm
P&O Heritage Ref. AC/02134/00
p. 10

HENRY FITZCOOK

From an album of watercolours
recording the Diorama of the *The
Route of the Overland Mail to India*
attributed to Henry Fitzcook (born
1824) and other hands, c.1850s

Detail from: *'Southampton Docks'*
Watercolour heightened with
bodycolour on paper
20.8 x 31.2 cm
P&O Heritage Ref. AC/02301/00
p. 9

Detail from: *'Mahmoudieh Canal'*
Watercolour and bodycolour on paper
20.8 x 31.3 cm
P&O Heritage Ref. AC/02313/00
p. 67

Detail from: *'The Central Station'*
Watercolour heightened with
white and bodycolour on paper
20.8 x 31.3 cm
P&O Heritage Ref. AC/02318/00
p. 69

Detail from: *'Encampment by night'*
Watercolour, bodycolour
heightened with white on paper
20.8 x 31.3 cm
P&O Heritage Ref. AC/02320/00
p. 70

'The Frontispiece'
Watercolour heightened with
bodycolour on paper
20.6 x 31.3 cm
P&O Heritage Ref. AC/02300/00
p. 214-215

Detail from: *'Cairo'*
Watercolour on paper heightened
with white and bodycolour on paper
20.8 x 31.3 cm
P&O Heritage Ref. AC/02315/00
p. 237

BERNARD FINEGAN GRIBBLE
1873-1962
RBC, RSMA

Morea in dry dock, c. 1919
Oil on canvas
95.6 x 65.7 cm
P&O Heritage Ref. AC/02092/00
p. 119

EDWARD HALLIDAY
1902-1984
CBE, RBA, RP, RA

Detail from: *Portrait of Sir William
Crawford Currie GBE*, 1960
(half length, seated)
Oil on canvas
100.3 x 74.9 cm
P&O Heritage Ref. AC/04171/00
p. 10

SIR GEORGE HAYTER
1792-1871

*Portrait of Lieutenant Thomas
Fletcher Waghorn RN*, 1844
(seated)
Oil on canvas

75.8 x 62.7 cm
P&O Heritage Ref. AC/01412/00
p. 66

DEREK HILL
1916-2000
CBE

Detail from: *Portrait of Sir Donald
Forsyth Anderson*, 1970 (seated)
Oil on canvas
62.5 x 75.3 cm
Private Collection
p. 10

WILLIAM AYERST INGRAM
1855-1913
RBA

Britannia coaling at night at Aden, c. 1895
Oil on canvas
101.6 x 180.5 cm
P&O Heritage Ref. AC/02982/00
p. 238-239

KUNITSURU
FL. 1870s

Detail from: *The P&O Office in
Yokohama, Naka Ku*, c. 1870s
Painted in watercolours
on silk laid on paper
33.4 x 85.2 cm
P&O Heritage Ref. AC/03282/00
p. 96-97

FRANK HENRY MASON
1876-1965
RSMA, RBA, RI

Baradine at sea, c. 1922
Gouache on board
61.1 x 54.2 cm
P&O Heritage Ref. AC/03014/00
p. 225

FRANK STEWART MURRAY
1848-1915

Detail from: *Valetta passing the
hulk of HMS Queen*, 1893
Watercolour heightened
with white on paper
57.4 x 131.2 cm
P&O Heritage Ref. AC/02115/00
p. 106

RICHARD HENRY NEVILLE-CUMMING
1843-1920

Victoria off Gibraltar, 1888
Watercolour and bodycolour on paper
56.7 x 46.6 cm

P&O Heritage Ref. AC/03173/00
p. 24

Ceylon *at anchor in the Thames
at Tilbury*, 1895
Gouache heightened with
white on board
46.1 x 95 cm
P&O Heritage Ref. AC/03531/00
p. 42

ANDREW NICHOLL
1804-1886
RHA

Off the coast of Gibraltar, c. 1847
Watercolour heightened
with white on paper
48.4 x 69.7 cm
P&O Heritage Ref. AC/03279/00
p. 58

Point de Galle, Ceylon, c. 1847
Watercolour over pencil with
some scratching out on paper
48.4 x 70 cm
P&O Heritage Ref. AC/03425/00
p. 81

CHARLES PEARS
1873-1958
PPSMA, ROI

Ranchi *in the Suez Canal*, c. 1925
Designed for an Empire
Marketing Board poster
Oil on canvas with pencil
96.5 x 146.7 cm
P&O Heritage Ref. AC/02119/00
p. 74

JOHN SINGER SARGENT
1856-1925

Detail from: *Portrait of Sir Thomas
Sutherland GCMG*, 1898
(three-quarter length, standing)
Oil on canvas
143.5 x 112.8 cm
P&O Heritage Ref. AC/02133/00
p. 10

STEPHEN DADD SKILLETT
1816-1866

Royal Tar *in rough seas*, 1838
Oil on canvas
59.1 x 79.9 cm
P&O Heritage Ref. AC/02020/00
p. 15

Braganza *off the English Coast*, 1837
Oil on canvas

51.7 x 74.7 cm
P&O Heritage Ref. AC/02099/00
p. 213

J. F. STACE

Pottinger *under sail and steam*, 1852
Oil on canvas
44.5 x 74.9 cm
P&O Heritage Ref. AC/03887/00
p. 93

RICHARD STONE
B.1951

Detail from: *Portrait of Lord Sterling
of Plaistow, GCVO, CBE*, 2006
(full length, standing)
Oil on canvas
152.2 cm x 101.1 cm
Gifted to the National Maritime
Museum by DP World
p. 10

WILLIAM ERIC THORP
1901-1993
PS, RSMA

Himalaya *leaving Tilbury
for the last time*, 1969
Oil on board with pencil
82 x 112.3 cm
P&O Heritage Ref. AC/02050/00
p. 45

NORMAN WILKINSON
1878-1971
CBE, PPRI, ROI, RSMA, HRWS

Stratheden *at anchor off Port Said*, 1937
Oil on canvas
74.9 x 111.7 cm
P&O Heritage Ref. AC/02935/00
p. 128-129

Rawalpindi *under fire in the
North Atlantic*, 1940
Oil on canvas
100.2 x 151.3 cm
P&O Heritage Ref. AC/02056/00
p. 226

WILLIAM LIONEL WYLLIE
1851-1931
RA, NEAC, RI, RBA, RPE

Detail from: Medina *departing for
the Royal Tour of India with King
George V and Queen Mary*, 1911
Oil on canvas
90.6 x 181.7 cm
P&O Heritage Ref. AC/02152/00
p. 171

Deck scene on board Peshawur, c. 1880s
Watercolour over pencil
heightened with bodycolour on
coloured paper laid on board
27.7 x 47.7 cm
P&O Heritage Ref. AC/03185/00
p. 180-181

ARTISTS UNATTRIBUTED

ANGLO-CHINESE SCHOOL

Oceana *at sea*, c. 1890
Oil on canvas (varnished)
43.6 x 58.2 cm
P&O Heritage Ref. AC/03187/00
p. 26

ARTIST UNKNOWN

*P&O Agent's house at Point
de Galle, Ceylon*, c. 1860s
Oil on board
34.5 x 52.6 cm
P&O Heritage Ref. AC/01714/00
p. 82

ARTIST UNKNOWN

*The P&O Office 'Tit Hong'
in Hong Kong*, c. 1855
Watercolour with fine pen and ink
(and some gouache) on paper
22.1 x 25.7 cm
P&O Heritage Ref. AC/02131/00
p. 91

PICTURE CREDITS

The authors and publishers gratefully
acknowledge the following individuals
and institutions for their kind permission
to reproduce the following images:

Richard Stone and the National
Maritime Museum (NMM) *p.10*;
Brian Webb *p. 27*; Patrick Rylands
p. 34; Naomi Games & the Estate of
Abram Games *p. 35 & 234*; © Briony
Campbell *p. 54*; © David Morris
p. 55; NMM *p.110*; Ulster Folk &
Transport Museum *p. 131*; Sydney
Morning Herald *p.162*; MOD/
Ministry of Defence *p.163*; © Press
Association *p. 172*; Coventry Evening
Telegraph *p.178*; © English Heritage
NMR *pp. 210, 219, 221*; Simon
Rendall & the Estate of E. McKnight
Kauffer *p. 234*.

All others images are from the P&O
Heritage Collection © P&OSNCo.
Commissioned photography by Marc
Walter: *pp.16-17, 65, 120-121,184,191,
216-217, 228-229 & 246-247*.

SELECTED SHIPS LIST

A complete listing of the P&O's historic fleet runs to over 1,000 ships and over 2,600 for the P&O group in its entirety. The following selected list includes only those vessels mentioned or illustrated in this book.

The ships are listed in alphabetical order by name (and where ships share the same name, in chronological order according to date of entry into service) and details given include: vessel type, gross tonnage (grt), P&O Group service dates and main employment. Unless otherwise stated the shipping line is P&O. For P&O group companies the following abbreviations are used: BI - British India Steam Navigation Company Ltd. and Orient Line - Orient Steam Navigation Company.

For further information about individual ships please refer to www.poheritage.com where 2,500 fact sheets are available to download.

ALMA
Passenger Liner
2,200 grt, 1855-1859
Egypt/India service

ARABIA (1898)
Passenger Liner
7,903 grt, 1898-1916
UK/India service

ARCADIA (1888)
Passenger Liner
6,610 grt, 1888-1915
UK/India and UK/
Australia services

ARCADIA (1954)
Passenger Liner
29,734 grt, 1954-1979
UK/Australia service
and cruising

ARDSHIEL (1969)
Tanker
119,678 grt, 1969-1977
Gulf/Europe or Gulf/Japan
'shuttle' services
Trident Tankers, then P&O

ASSAM (1873)
Passenger Liner
3,033 grt, 1875-1895
India/Australia and
Italy/India services

AUSTRALIA (1892)
Passenger Liner
6.901 grt, 1892-1904
UK/Australia service

AZOF (1855)
Paddle Steamer
700 grt, 1856-1871
Yemen/Mauritius and
later China Coast services

BALLARAT (1911)
Passenger Liner
11,120 grt, 1911-1917
UK/Australia emigrant service

BALRANALD (1922)
Passenger Liner
13,039 grt, 1922-1936
UK/Australia emigrant service

BARADINE (1921)
Passenger Liner
13,144, grt, 1921-1936
UK/Australia emigrant service

BENARES (1858)
Passenger Liner
1,491 grt, 1858-1868
Egypt/Australia, later Egypt/India
and then India/Far East services

BENDIGO (1922)
Passenger Liner
13,039 grt, 1922-1936
UK/Australia emigrant service

BENTINCK (1843)
Paddle Steamer
1,800 grt, 1843-1860
Egypt/India service

BRAGANZA (1836)
Paddle Steamer
688 grt, 1837-1852
UK/Spain and Portugal,
later UK/ Black Sea,
then India/Far East services

BRITANNIA (1887)
Passenger Liner
6,061 grt, 1887-1909
UK/Australia, UK/India
and UK/Far East services

CALEDONIA (1894)
Passenger Liner
7,558 grt, 1894-1925
UK/India service

CANBERRA (1961)
Passenger Liner
45,720 grt, 1961-1997

UK/Australasia and
Pacific service, and cruising

CARNATIC (1863)
Passenger Liner
2,014 grt, 1863-1869
Egypt/India service

CARTHAGE (1881)
Passenger Liner
5,013 grt, 1881-1903
UK/Australia service

CEYLON (1894)
Passenger Liner
4.094 grt, 1894-1913
UK/ Far East service

CHINA (1896)
Passenger Liner
7,912 grt, 1896-1928
UK/India and UK/
Australia services

CHITRAL (1925)
Passenger Liner
15,248 grt, 1925-1953
UK/Australia service

CHUSAN (1852)
Passenger Liner
750 grt, 1852-1861
Singapore/Australia later India/
Far East services

CHUSAN (1950)
Passenger Liner
24,215 grt, 1950-1973
UK/Far East service, and cruising

COLOMBO (1853)
Passenger Liner
1,800 grt, 1853-1862
UK/Egypt, later East
of Suez services

DELHI (1905)
Passenger Liner
8,090 grt, 1905-1911
UK/India and China service

DELTA (1867)
Passenger Liner
1,618 grt, 1859-1874
France/Egypt service

DELTA (1905)
Passenger Liner
8,053 grt, 1905-1929
China service

DEVONIA (1939)
Educational Cruise Ship

12,796 grt, 1962-1967
Educational cruising
BI

DON JUAN (1837)
Paddle Steamer
932 grt, 1837-1837
UK/Spain and Portugal service

DOURO (1853)
Passenger/Cargo Liner
810 grt, 1853-1854
India/China service

DUNERA (1937)
Troopship, later Educational Cruise Ship
11,161 grt, 1937-1967
Trooping, and after 1961
educational cruising
BI

EGYPT (1897)
Passenger Liner
7,912 grt, 1897-1922
UK/Australia and UK/India services

ELK (1977)
Roll-on/roll-off Cargo Ferry
5,463 gt, 1977-2000
UK/Sweden service
P&O Ferries

HIMALAYA (1854)
Passenger Liner
3,438 grt, 1854 then sold
UK/Egypt service

HIMALAYA (1892)
Passenger Liner
6,898 grt, 1892-1916 and 1919-1922
UK/Australia and later UK/
India and UK/China services

HIMALAYA (1949)
Passenger Liner
27,955 grt, 1949-1974
UK/Australia service, and cruising

HINDOSTAN (1842)
Passenger Liner
1,800 grt, 1842-1864
UK/India service

IBERIA (1836)
Paddle Steamer
516 grt, 1836-1896
UK/Spain and Portugal service

IBERIA (1954)
Passenger Liner
29,614 grt, 1954-1972
UK/Australia service

INDIA (1896)
Passenger Liner
7,911 grt, 1896-1915
UK/India and UK/
Australia services

KAISAR-I-HIND (1878)
Passenger Liner
4,023 grt, 1878-1897
UK/India service

LADY MARY WOOD (1842)
Paddle Steamer
650 grt, 1842-1858
UK/Spain and Portugal, later India/
Far East and China Coast services

LIVERPOOL (1830)
Paddle Steamer
330 grt, 1835-1845
UK/Spain and Portugal service

MACEDONIA (1904)
Passenger Liner
10,552 grt, 1906-1931
UK/Australia and UK/
India and Far East services

MALOJA (1911)
Passenger Liner
12,431 grt, 1911-1916
UK/Australia service

MALOJA (1923)
Passenger Liner
20.837grt, 1923-1954
UK/Australia service

MANTUA (1909)
Passenger Liner
10,885 grt, 1909-1935
UK/Australia and UK/
India services

MARMORA (1903)
Passenger Liner
10,509 grt, 1903-1916 / 1917-1918
UK/Australia service

MASSILIA (1884)
Passenger Liner
4,902 grt, 1884-1903
UK/Australia and UK/
Far East services

MEDINA (1911)
Passenger Liner
12,350 grt, 1911-1917
UK/Australia service

MIRZAPORE (1871)
Passenger Liner
3,763 grt, 1871-1897

UK/India and UK/
Far East services

MOLDAVIA (1903)
Passenger Liner
9,500 grt, 1903-1916 / 1917-1918
UK/Australia service

MOLDAVIA (1922)
Passenger Liner
16,543 grt, 1922-1938
UK/Australia service

MONGOLIA (1903)
Passenger Liner
9,505 grt, 1903-1917
UK/Australia service

MONGOLIA (1923)
Passenger Liner
20,847 grt, 1923-1954
UK/Australia service

MOREA (1908)
Passenger Liner
10,890 grt, 1908-1930
UK/Australia or UK/
India services

NARKUNDA (1920)
Passenger Liner
16,227 grt, 1920-1942
UK/Australia service

NEVASA (1956)
Troopship, later Educational
Cruise Ship
20,527 grt, 1956-1975
Trooping and after 1965
educational cruising
BI

NORLAND (1974)
Roll on/Roll off Passenger Ferry
12,988 grt, 1974-2002
UK/Holland, then UK/
Belgium services
North Sea Ferries Ltd., P&O

OCEANA (1888)
Passenger Liner
6,610 grt, 1888-1912
UK/Australia and UK/India services

ORIANA (1960)
Passenger Liner
41,915 grt, 1960-1986
UK/Australasia and Pacific
services, and cruising
Orient Line, P&O

ORIENTAL (1840)
Paddle Steamer

1,673 grt, 1840-1861
UK/Egypt then Egypt/
India services

ORION (1935)
Passenger Liner
23,371 grt, 1935-1963
UK/Australia service and cruising
Orient Line

ORONSAY (1951)
Passenger Liner
27,632 grt, 1951-1975
UK/Australia service and cruising
Orient Line

PARRAMATTA (1882)
Passenger Liner
4,771 grt, 1882-1903
UK/Australia and UK/
Far East services

PEKIN (1847)
Paddle Steamer
1,200 grt, 1847-1869
India/Hong Kong service

PEKIN (1871)
Passenger Liner
3,777 grt, 1871-1897
UK/India and UK/Far East services

PERSIA (1900)
Passenger Liner
7,951 grt, 1900-1915
UK/India service

PESHAWUR (1871)
Passenger Liner
3,782 grt, 1871-1900
UK/India, Far East
or Australia services

PLASSY (1901)
Passenger/Cargo Ship; Troopship
7,342 grt, 1901-1924
Troopship, hospital ship and
"intermediate" passenger services

POTTINGER (1846)
Paddle Steamer
1.300 grt, 1846-1867
India/China service

PRECURSOR (1841)
Passenger Liner
1,600 grt, 1844-1869
Eygpt/India service

RAJPUTANA (1925)
Passenger Liner
16,568 grt, 1925-1941
UK/India, later UK/Far East services

RANCHI (1925)
Passenger Liner
16,650 grt, 1925-1953
UK/India service and cruising. Post-
war emigrant service UK/Australia

RANPURA (1925)
Passenger Liner
16,601 grt, 1925-1944
UK/India, later UK/
Far East services

RAWALPINDI (1925)
Passenger Liner
16,619 grt, 1925-1939
UK/India, later UK/
Far East services

RAZMAK (1925)
Passenger Liner
10,602 grt, 1925-1960
Yemen/India shuttle service

ROME (1881)
Passenger Liner,
later Cruising Yacht
5,010 grt, 1881-1912
UK/Australia service; cruising
from 1904 as VECTIS

ROYAL TAR (1832)
Passenger Liner
308 grt, 1834-1847
UK/Spain and Portugal service

SIMLA (1894)
Passenger/Cargo Liner and Troopship
5,884 grt, 1894-1916
UK/India service and trooping

SOCOTRA (1943)
General Cargo Liner
7,840 grt, 1943-1965
UK/ Ceylon and UK/
India services

STRATHAIRD (1932)
Passenger Liner
22,544 grt, 1932-1961
UK/Australia service

STRATHALLAN (1938)
Passenger Liner
23,722 grt, 1938-1942
UK/Australia service and cruising

STRATHEDEN (1937)
Passenger Liner
23,722 grt, 1937-1964
UK/Australia service and cruising

STRATHMORE (1935)
Passenger Liner

23,428 grt, 1935-1963
UK/Australia service and cruising

STRATHNAVER (1931)
Passenger Liner
22,547 grt, 1931-1962
UK/Australia service and cruising

SURAT (1866)
Passenger Liner
2,578 grt, 1866-1894
Egypt/India, later UK/India
and Italy/India services

SURAT (1948)
General Cargo Liner
8.925 grt, 1948-1972
UK/ Northern Europe and UK/
Far East

SUMATRA (1867)
Passenger Liner
2,202 grt, 1867-1886
Far Eastern services

SYRIA (1901)
Passenger/Cargo Liner
6,660 grt, 1901-1924
UK/India and UK/China
intermediate services, and trooping

TAGUS (1837)
Paddle Steamer
909 grt, 1837-1864
UK/Spain and Portugal and
UK/Black Sea services

UGANDA (1952)
Passenger Liner; Educational

Cruise Ship
14,430 grt, 1952-1986
UK/East Africa service and
after 1967 educational cruising
BI

VALETTA (1853)
Paddle Steamer
900 grt, 1853-1865
France/Egypt service

VALETTA (1884)
Passenger Liner
4,904 grt, 1884-1903
UK/Australia and UK/
Far East services

VECTIS (1881) FORMERLY ROME
Passenger Liner; Cruising Yacht

5,010 grt, 1881-1912
UK/Australia service and
cruising from 1904

VICEROY OF INDIA (1929)
Passenger Liner
19,648 grt, 1929-1942
UK/India service and cruising

VICTORIA (1887)
Passenger Liner
6,091 grt, 1887-1909
UK/Australia, UK/India
and UK/Far East services

WILLIAM FAWCETT (1828)
Paddle Steamer
206 grt, 1835-1840
UK/Spain and Portugal service

'If you are ever shipwrecked, my dearest Laura…do contrive to get the catastrophe conducted by the Peninsular and Oriental Company…. I believe other companies drown you sometimes; and drowning is a very prosaic arrangement…fit only for seafaring people and second-class passengers. I have just been shipwrecked under the auspices of the P. and O., and I assure you that it is the pleasantest thing imaginable. It has its little hardships, to be sure; but so has a picnic; and the wreck was one of the most agreeable picnics you can imagine.'

MRS DULCIMER, 1863

QUOTATION REFERENCES

Full references for quotations cited in the text are listed in alphabetical order by author or where necessary by publication. Where applicable, references are given to documents held in the P&O Heritage Collection and marked as 'P&O Heritage' or 'P&O Archive'. To consult the 'P&O Archive' references please contact the National Maritime Museum, Greenwich where the Company's archive is accessible to the public.

Please note: Page numbers given refer to this publication.

Adamson, Sir William, letters to his father from *Himalaya*, 1854 (P&O Archive Ref. P&O/092/001) (pp.76, 107, 144, 166, 183, 184, 189) [Sir William Adamson was P&O Director from 1893 until 1917.]

American Passenger quoted at the *P&O Annual General Meeting*, 8th December 1937 (P&O Archive Ref. P&O/006) (p.84)

Anderson, Arthur, *Special Report Containing Letters from the Original Managing Directors of the Peninsular & Oriental Steam Navigation Company and Statements made by them at the Half-Yearly Meeting of the Proprietors*, 12th June 1854 (pp.211, 216); 'Statement to the Post Office Reform Committee', 1838, cited in John Nicolson, *Arthur Anderson: A Founder of the P&O Company* (Lerwick: T. & J. Manson, 1932) (pp.11, 12, 14)

Anderson, Sir Colin, *Architectural Review*, June 1967 (p.114)

Anderson, Sir Donald, letter to Sir Hugh Casson, dated 25th October 1960 (p.130)

Anonymous homeward bound passenger on board *Viceroy of India*, c. 1930s (p.190)

Anonymous passenger on board *Pekin*, 1891, cited in Peter Padfield, *Beneath the House Flag of the P&O* (London: Hutchinson, 1981) (p.166)

Anonymous traveller cited in Boyd Cable (Colonel Ernest Andrew

Ewart), *A Hundred Year History of the P&O* (London: Ivor Nicholson and Watson, 1937) (p.68)

Anson, Miss, letter to the P&O Directors, 1890s (P&O Archive Ref. P&O/065/209) (p.166)

Arnold, Sir Edwin, *India Revisited* (London: Kegan Paul, Trench, Trübner, & Co. Ltd., 1899) (pp.72, 157, 201-202)

Artmonsky, Ruth, *Shipboard Style, Colin Anderson of the Orient Line* (London: Artmonsky Arts, 2010) (p.136)

Asher, Mrs D., on board *Strathallan* with the Queen Alexandra's Imperial Military Nursing Service in 1942 (p.163)

Athenaeum, 9th March 1907 (p.223)

Attiwill, Kenneth, *The Singapore Story* (London: Frederick Muller, 1959) (p.87)

Author known by pseudonym 'A P&O', *Always Ready or Every One his Pride*, (London: Hall, Virtue & Co., 1859) (p.7)

Baillie, Captain D.G.H.O., *A Sea Affair* (London: Hutchinson, 1957) (p.141, 144, 160, 163, 166); 'The Overland Mail at Marseilles', *About Ourselves*, January 1953 (pp.61, 62, 64, 84) [Captain Baillie joined P&O as a cadet rising to Commodore during his 40 year career with the Company.]

Bigsby, Lena, letters from *Macedonia* dated c. 1910 (P&O Archive Ref. P&O/092/009) (pp.151, 157, 184, 205)

Biheller, Walter, letters to his fiancée from *China*, dated 1927 (P&O Archive Ref. P&O/092/015) (pp.192, 194, 205)

Birk, Alma, 'Thanks for the tip', *Maiden Voyage*, *Canberra* Souvenir Brochure, 1961 (P&O Heritage Ref. AC/08105/00) (p.134)

Black, Misha, 'Décor that Shapes the Future', *Maiden Voyage*, *Canberra* Souvenir Brochure,

1961 (P&O Heritage Ref. AC/08105/00) (p.103)

Blackwood's Edinburgh Magazine, 'English Embassies to China' January 1861, Vol. 89 (p.92)

Bolitho, Hector, *James Lyle Mackay, First Earl of Inchcape* (London: John Murray, 1936) (Reprinted by kind permission of John Murray Publishers) (p.27)

Bridge, Captain G., 'Landing Passengers at Tilbury', *About Ourselves*, December 1952 (p.44) [Captain Bridge was P&O's Dock Superintendent at Tilbury.]

Buggé, Olaf Leganger, 'Closed but not Forgotten', *Wavelength*, March 1973 (pp.50 & 52); 'In memory of number 122', *Wavelength*, October/November 1979 (p.46) [Buggé began his P&O career as shore staff in the late 1920s.]

Cable, Boyd (Colonel Ernest Andrew Ewart), 'Sea Heraldry', *The Times*, 7th September 1937 (p.244)

Calwell, Arthur, address given in 1945 as Australian Minister for Immigration (p.101)

Casson, Sir Hugh, letter to John West, dated 18th October 1960 (p.130); *Maiden Voyage*, *Canberra* Souvenir Brochure, 1961 (P&O Heritage Ref. AC/08105/00) (p.130)

Colomb, Captain Philip RN, 1868, later Admiral, cited in Peter Padfield, *Beneath the House Flag of the P&O* (London: Hutchinson, 1981) (p.183)

Coward, Sir Noël, 'P.& O. 1930', *Noël Coward Collected Verse*, Ed. Payn, Graham and Tickner, Martin (London: Methuen Drama, 1984) (p.169, 209) (Reproduced by kind permission of Bloomsbury Publishing Plc. © Sir Noël Coward)

Cushing, Hon. Caleb, American Commissioner to China, *Illustrated London News*, 1844 (p.76)

Crichton, Sir Andrew, *Recollections of Early Business Life* (London: P&O,

1986) (pp.31, 52, 76, 87); *Further Recollections of Early Business Life* (London: P&O, 1986) (p.95) [Sir Andrew Crichton joined P&O in 1929 becoming Managing Director in 1957 until 1966. He was Chairman of OCL 1965-1973, and remained on the board of Directors of P&O until his retirement in 1981.]

Diary of a Java-bound Engineer travelling in 1846 (P&O Archive Ref. P&O/073/002) (pp.8, 68, 76, 104, 143)

Dulcimer, Mrs, 'Mrs Dulcimer's Shipwreck, a Lady's narrative addressed to a friend', November 1863, in Blanchard, Sidney Laman, *Yesterday and To-day in India*, (London: William. H. Allen & Co., 1867) (p.254)

Dyer, L., postcard from *Salsette* (P&O Heritage Ref. PC/0437/00) (p.176)

Earle, Harriet, cited in Annabel Venning, *Following the Drum, The Lives of Army Wives and Daughters* (London: Headline, 2006) (p.187)

Evening Standard, 11th October 1889 (p.173)

Ford, Helen, 1888, cited in Peter Padfield, *Beneath the House Flag of the P&O* (London: Hutchinson, 1981) (p.43)

Furlong, Captain G. H., *The Bendigo Log*, Ed. White, W. North, 1924, (P&O Archive Ref. P&O/092/013) (p.183) [Captain Furlong joined P&O in 1896 on board the *Peninsular*. Amongst the many ships he served on he was Chief Officer on board *Medina* and in 1924 took command of *Bendigo*.]

Furniss, Harry, *P&O Sketches in Pen and Ink*, 1898 (pp.61, 75, 84, 194, 202)

Gordon-Cumming, c. 1860s, cited in Peter Padfield, *Beneath the House Flag of the P&O* (London: Hutchinson, 1981) (p.80)

Graham, Gerald, *A Concise History of the British Empire* (London: Thames & Hudson Ltd., © 1971) (Reprinted by kind permission of Thames & Hudson Ltd., London) (p.57)

Grimshaw, Beatrice, 'Under the Southern Cross', *P&O Pocket Book*, 1926 (P&O Heritage Ref. AC/04961/00) (back cover)

Harley, Jack, 'A Letter from Aden' *About Ourselves*, September 1953 (p.79) [Jack Harley worked at the P&O Agency in Aden in the early 1920s]

Heaton, J. Henniker, letter to Sir Thomas Sutherland dated December 1913 (P&O Archive Ref. P&O/065/213) (p.57)

Henderson, George, diary written on board *Rome* and *China* in 1901 (P&O Archive Ref. P&O/092/010) (pp.151, 192, 196, 206)

Hervey, Albert Henry Andrew, *The Ocean and the Desert by a Madras Officer, Vol. 1* (London: T. C. Newby, 1846) (pp.68, 83, 104, 107, 189, 205) [Hervey travelled on board *Hindostan* from India to Suez.]

Howarth, David and Stephen, *The Story of P&O* (London: George Weidenfeld & Nicolson Ltd., 1986) © P&OSNCo (p.34)

Illustrated London News, Obituary of Richard Bourne, 1st November 1851 (p.19); 22nd May 1852 (p.39)

Inchcape, Lord (first Earl), *Agenda for P&O Board meeting*, 29th April 1925, (P&O Archive Ref. P&O/001/001) (p.118); *P&O Annual Report of the Board of Directors*, 8th December 1915 (P&O Archive Ref. P&O/006) (p.21); *P&O Seventy-Sixth Ordinary General Meeting*, 13th December 1916 (P&O Archive Ref. P&O/006) (p.165); *Report of the proceedings at the Eighty-Third General Meeting of the Proprietors*, 12th December 1923 (P&O Archive Ref. P&O/006) (p.28); *The Times*, January 7th 1922 (p.25)

Inchcape, Lord (third Earl), *Chairman's Statement*, relating to Annual Report for 1978, 2nd May 1979 (p.34)

Interior Design, 'P&O Offices London', July 1972 (p.233)

Johnson, W.F. Law, letter to his mother during his service at the P&O Agency in Aden, dated 23rd September 1919 (p.76) [Johnson worked for P&O from 1913 to 1960]

Jones, Stephanie, 'The P&O in War & Slump, 1914-1932: the Chairmanship of Lord Inchcape' in *Innovation in Shipping and Trade*, Ed. Fisher, Stephen (Exeter: University of Exeter, 1989) (p.27)

Journalist on board *Arcadia*, c. 1890, cited in Peter Padfield, *Beneath the House Flag of the P&O*, (London: Hutchinson, 1981) (p.110)

Kendall, Franklin Richardson, letters to his mother dated 1858-1866 (P&O Archive Ref. P&O/091/008) (pp.57, 88, 90, 103) [Kendall joined P&O in 1856, first working in P&O's overseas agencies. He remained with the Company for 50 years and reached the position of Chief General Manager.]

Kipling, Rudyard, *The Exiles' Line*, 1890 (p.170); letter to Charles Scribner dated 21st March 1932 in *The Letters of Rudyard Kipling, Volume 6: 1931-36*, Ed. Pinney, Thomas (London: Palgrave Macmillan, 2004) (Reprinted by kind permission of Macmillan Publishers Ltd.) (p.170)

Lady Lisbeth, 'Mediterranean outfit for April', *The Queen, The Lady's Newspaper & Court Chronicle*, 16th February 1895 (P&O Archive Ref. P&O/098/053) (p.194)

Lady traveller on board *Hindostan*, 1844 (P&O Archive Ref. P&O/065/157) (p.104)

Leighton, Lord, letter to his father dated 1873 (Reprinted by kind permission of the Leighton House Collection, CH.1/5/33i) (p.240)

Lloyd's List, 'Last Word: Office work of art', 1st February 2011 (p.54) © Lloyd's List

Manser, Michael, 'Breakthrough for Commerce in the Dreary City', *Design Magazine*, June 1970 (pp.234, 236)

Melville, T. A., in *One Hundred Years of Singapore*, Ed. Makepeace, Walter etc. (London: John Murray, 1921) (p.87)

Morning Post, 12th May 1898 (p.220)

Mostert, Noël, *Supership* (London: Penguin Books Ltd., 1976) (Reprinted by kind permission of Penguin Books Ltd.) (p.151)

Nicolson, John, *Arthur Anderson: A Founder of the P&O Company* (Lerwick: T. & J. Manson, 1932) (p.49)

Ondaatje, Michael, *The Cat's Table* (London: Jonathan Cape, 2011) (Reprinted by kind permission of The Random House Group Limited) (p.173)

P&O Annual Report, 30th November 1842 (p.72); 30th September 1874 (p.19) (both P&O Archive Ref. P&O/006)

P&O Board Minutes, 25th July 1843 (P&O Archive Ref. P&O/001) (p.211)

P&O Brochure, *The Pleasure Cruises of the P&O Company*, part of a bound selection of P&O brochures and publicity material for 1910 (P&O Heritage Ref. AC/04573/00) (p.223)

P&O Circulars, January 1871 (p.187); August 1872 (p.146) (both P&O Archive Ref. P&O/007)

P&O Guide Book for Passengers, printed for the Royal Naval Exhibition, 1891 (P&O Archive Ref. P&O/091/022) (p.98)

P&O House Magazine, *About Ourselves*, 'P&O Museum', 1952 (pp.227, 230); 'Reflections of a Passage Clerk', December 1952 (pp.49, 50); 'The Publicity Department', March 1954 (p.234); 1956 (p.245)

P&O Instructions for Chief Engineers, 1867 (P&O Archive

Ref. P&O/009/001) (p.146)

P&O Instructions for Pursers, Clerks and Stewards, 1860 (P&O Archive Ref. P&O/010/010) (pp.147, 183)

P&O Mail Contract, 1853 (P&O Archive Ref. P&O/30) (p.146)

P&O Managing Directors, in a letter to recipients of *Rawalpindi* framed print (P&O Archive Ref. P&O/065/286) (p.227)

P&O on board publication, *Himalaya Observer*, 2nd May 1896, (London: Printed for private circulation by Boot, Son & Carpenter) (paraphrased in Peter Padfield, *Beneath the House Flag of the P&O* (London: Hutchinson, 1981)) (pp.189, 192)

P&O on board publication, *Marmora Gazette*, February 1912 (P&O Archive Ref. P&O/065/207) (p.192)

P&O publication, *Men of the Ships*, 'Keeping the ship in shape' (London: P&O, 1960) (p.152)

Peninsular Steam Navigation Company, *Prospectus*, August 1834 (The British Library) (p.12)

Peninsular Steam Navigation Company, dummy advertisement in *The Shetland Journal*, 2nd January 1837 (p.103)

Randall, Ashley, 'Now and Then', *About Ourselves*, Summer 1971 (p.112); *Wavelength*, August 1973 (pp.50, 52) [Randall joined P&O aged 18 in 1905 and stayed with the Company for 24 years.]

Rawdin, Edward, *Three Months in the Mediterranean: Notes on a Cruise in the P&O Company's Steam Yacht 'Vectis'*, (London, 1905) (P&O Archive Ref. P&O/092/011) (pp.116 & 118, 199, 205, 206)

Reynolds, Fred, on board *India*, 1896 (P&O Archive Ref. P&O/065) (pp.157, 196, 201)

Scarborough Gazette, 'Life on an Ocean Steamer', 9th February 1888 (pp.110 & 112, 184, 187, 202)

Shaw, The Rt Hon Alexander, (later Second Baron Craigmyle) letter to staff on his appointment as P&O Chairman, dated 8th June 1932 (p.31)

Smith, Right Reverend G. V., Bishop of Willesden, Service in commemoration of the P&O Centenary, 14th October 1937, *A Souvenir of a Century of the Peninsular & Oriental Steam Navigation Company* (P&O Archive Ref. P&O/091/081) (pp.33, 157)

Soldier of 2/4th Infantry Battalion of the Second A.I.F. on board *Strathnaver* writing in the *Sydney Morning Herald*, 10th January 1950 (p.163)

Starling, Edith, *Rawalpindi*, 1938, cited in Peter Padfield, *Beneath the House Flag of the P&O* (London: Hutchinson, 1981) (p.202)

Steele, Captain Gordon Charles, VC, RN, 'My First Passenger Liner', *About Ourselves*, June 1957 (pp.141, 144)

Sterling, Lord, speeches made in 1983 (p.11); 1992 (p.90); on board *Oriana*, April 5th 1995 (p.37); *Annual General Meeting*, 13th May 2004 (p.37)

Sutherland, Sir Thomas, *Annual General Meeting*, 8th December 1915 (P&O Archive Ref. P&O/006) (p.25); *P&O Pocket Book*, 1888-9 (P&O Heritage Ref. AC/02782/00) (pp.71, 72, 95); *Report of the proceedings of the Annual General Meeting*, 13th December 1910 (P&O Archive Ref. P&O/006) (pp.166, 245)

Symonds, Captain Sir William, RN, extract from a letter dated July 1841 (P&O Archive Ref. P&O/065) (p.103)

Thackeray, William Makepeace, *Notes of a journey from Cornhill to Grand Cairo* (Heathfield: Cockbird Press Ltd., 1846) (pp.58, 68, 144, 147, 166 & 170, 201)

The Morning Chronicle, 22nd October 1850 (p.213)

The Southampton Times, 25th February, 1893 (p.44)

The Times, 8th November 1862 (p.40); 17th August 1935 (P&O Archive Ref. OSN/015/007) (pp.127 & 130)

Turner, Joseph Mallord William, exhibiting at the Royal Academy of Arts in 1842 (p.240)

Twain, Mark, extract from his diary on board *Oceana*, 1895 to 1896 (University of California, Berkeley) (p.170)

Twynam, Sir William, *The First P&O Voyage to The East*, (Ceylon: A. C. M. Press, 1916) (P&O Heritage Ref. AC/05402/00) (pp.76 & 83, 157, 187)

Vernon Gibbs, Commander C. R., *British Passenger Liners of the Five Oceans*, (London: G. P.Putnam's Sons, 1963) (Reprinted by kind permission of Penguin Books Ltd.) (p.242)

Waghorn, Lieutenant Thomas, cited in Boyd Cable (Colonel Ernest Andrew Ewart) *A Hundred Year History of the P&O* (London: Ivor Nicholson and Watson, 1937) (p.68)

Watkin-Thomas, M., 'Our Asian Crews', *About Ourselves*, September 1955 (pp.151 & 154, 154)

Watts, Mrs M. A., diaries written on board *Arcadia*, 1963 (P&O Archive Ref. P&O/092/017) (kindly donated by Mrs Watts' son, Mr Paul Madge)(pp.147, 174, 202, 206)

Whistler, J. M., 1900, writing to Miss R. Birnie Philip in the Correspondence of James McNeill Whistler, 1855-1903 (Whistler Manuscript Collection, MS Whistler P422) (Reprinted with kind permission of the University of Glasgow Library, Department of Special Collections) (p.240)

White, W. North, Ed. *The Bendigo Log*, 1924 (P&O Archive Ref. P&O/092/013) (pp.147, 201)

Wilkinson, Norman, *A Brush with Life* (London: Seeley Service & Co. Ltd., 1969) (pp.223, 224, 227)

Willcox, Brodie McGhie, *Special Report after the Half-Yearly General Meeting*, 12th June 1854 (p.19)

INDEX

The end, and to most people, the only sad part of the voyage
has come at last, though two of our friends, at least
have determined to stick to, the good old motto

Quis Separabit ..

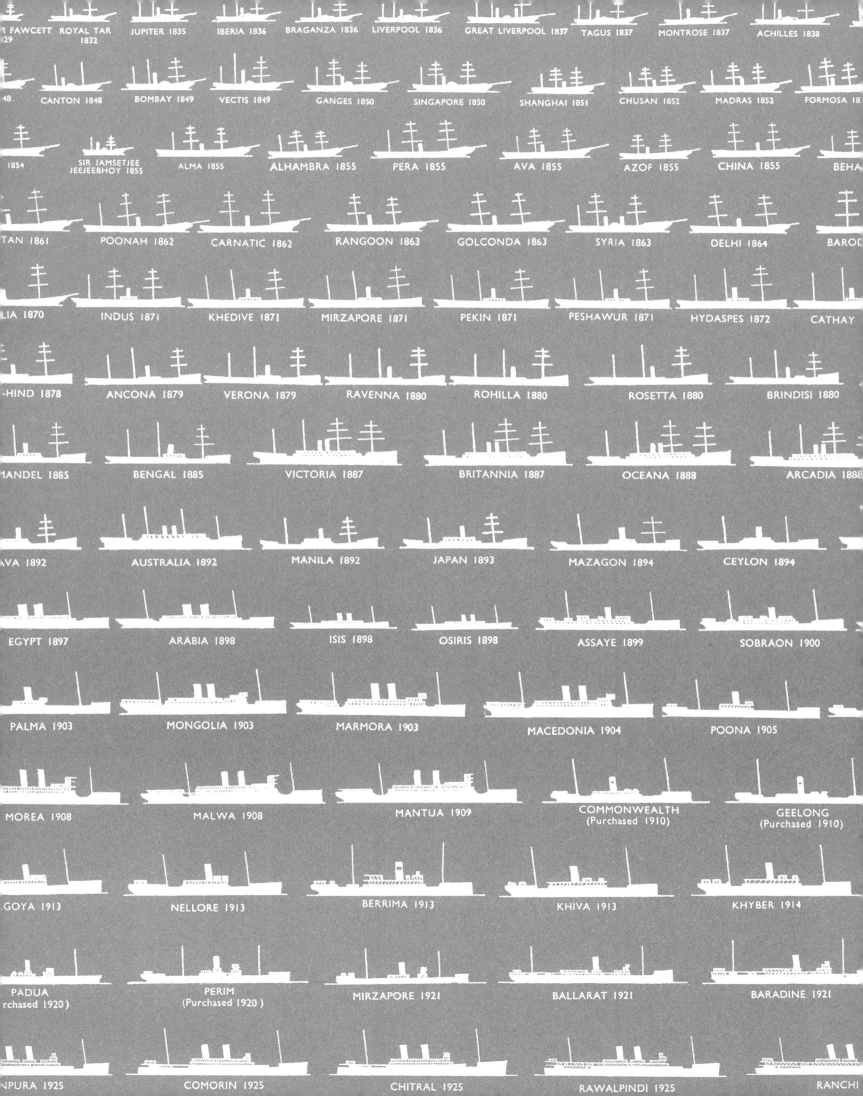

FAWCETT ROYAL TAR 1832 JUPITER 1835 IBERIA 1836 BRAGANZA 1836 LIVERPOOL 1836 GREAT LIVERPOOL 1837 TAGUS 1837 MONTROSE 1837 ACHILLES 1838

48. CANTON 1848 BOMBAY 1849 VECTIS 1849 GANGES 1850 SINGAPORE 1850 SHANGHAI 1851 CHUSAN 1852 MADRAS 1852 FORMOSA 18

1854 SIR JAMSETJEE JEEJEEBHOY 1855 ALMA 1855 ALHAMBRA 1855 PERA 1855 AVA 1855 AZOF 1855 CHINA 1855 BEHA

TAN 1861 POONAH 1862 CARNATIC 1862 RANGOON 1863 GOLCONDA 1863 SYRIA 1863 DELHI 1864 BAROD

LIA 1870 INDUS 1871 KHEDIVE 1871 MIRZAPORE 1871 PEKIN 1871 PESHAWUR 1871 HYDASPES 1872 CATHAY

-HIND 1878 ANCONA 1879 VERONA 1879 RAVENNA 1880 ROHILLA 1880 ROSETTA 1880 BRINDISI 1880

MANDEL 1885 BENGAL 1885 VICTORIA 1887 BRITANNIA 1887 OCEANA 1888 ARCADIA 1888

VA 1892 AUSTRALIA 1892 MANILA 1892 JAPAN 1893 MAZAGON 1894 CEYLON 1894

EGYPT 1897 ARABIA 1898 ISIS 1898 OSIRIS 1898 ASSAYE 1899 SOBRAON 1900

PALMA 1903 MONGOLIA 1903 MARMORA 1903 MACEDONIA 1904 POONA 1905

MOREA 1908 MALWA 1908 MANTUA 1909 COMMONWEALTH (Purchased 1910) GEELONG (Purchased 1910)

GOYA 1913 NELLORE 1913 BERRIMA 1913 KHIVA 1913 KHYBER 1914

PADUA (Purchased 1920) PERIM (Purchased 1920) MIRZAPORE 1921 BALLARAT 1921 BARADINE 1921

NPURA 1925 COMORIN 1925 CHITRAL 1925 RAWALPINDI 1925 RANCHI

A 1839 ORIENTAL 1840 PRECURSOR 1841 LADY MARY WOOD 1842 HINDOSTAN 1842 PACHA 1842 BENTINCK 1843 DELTA 1844 MADRID 1845 TIBER

BOMBAY 1852 BENGAL 1853 CADIZ 1853 VALETTA 1853 VECTIS 1853 RAJAH 1853 TARTAR 1853 DOURO 1853 NO

855 COLUMBIAN 1855 ELLORA 1855 ADEN 1856 ORISSA 1856 GRANADA 1857 NEMESIS 1857 MALABAR 1858

1864 COREA 1864 NYANZA 1864 MONGOLIA 1865 NIPHON 1865 TANJORE 1865 GEELONG 1866 AVOCA 1866

2 MALWA 1873 VENETIA 1873 BOKHARA 1873 ASSAM 1873 LOMBARDY 1873 ZAMBESI 1873 GWALIOR 18

VECTIS 1904 née ROME 1881 CLYDE 1881 CARTHAGE 1881 SHANNON 1881 GANGES 1882 THAMES 1882

PENINSULAR 1888 NANKIN 1888 TIENTSIN 1888 PEKIN 1888 ORIENTAL 1889 BOMBAY

CALEDONIA 1894 SIMLA 1894 NUBIA 1895 MALTA 1895 BORNEO 1895 SUMATRA

BANCA 1900 PERSIA 1900 PLASSY 1900 SICILIA 1901 SOUDAN 1901

ESHAWUR 1905 DELTA 1905 MOOLTAN 1905 DONGOLA 1905 DELHI 1905 D

NARRUNG (Purchased 1910) WAKOOL (Purchased 1910) WILCANNIA (Purchased 1910) MEDINA 1911 MALOJA 191

BORDA 1914 KAISAR-I-HIND 1914 KASHGAR 1914 KASHMIR 1914 KARMALA

BARRABOOL 1923 BALRANALD 1923 BENDIGO 1923 MOLDAVIA 1923

925 RAJPUTANA 1925 VICEROY OF INDIA 1929 SOMALI 1930 SOUDAN